PRAIS

I have known Bo Williams for most of my adult life and his witness has always been saturated with grace. This book is from a life well-lived. May you discover new revelations of God's goodness on every page.

Brady Boyd
Senior Pastor, New Life Church, Colorado Springs
Author of *Addicted to Busy*

Bo Williams and I have been friends for over forty years. For many years, we worked closely as elders and pastors at Trinity Fellowship Church. I can tell you that this book comes from the heart of a true man of God. What is written in this book is represented in the life, marriage, family and ministry of Bo Williams. I highly recommend this book for anyone who desires a biblical and balanced understanding on the subject of God's grace.

Jimmy Evans
Founder and President, XO Marriage

Very few people I have ever encountered have a love of scripture with the intensity that Bo does. My salvation was the day I became a new man, but the day Bo began teaching me what it truly means to be a new man is the day I truly stepped into the acceptance of the profound and indescribable gift of grace. One of the most misunderstood theological truths—now becomes accessible and actionable through this compelling book.

Josh Morris
Founder, Tov Co
www.tov.co

ii | NEW: ALREADY & BECOMING

Bo Williams first opened our eyes years ago to the reality of grace and the depths of Jesus Christ's accomplishment on the cross, and it has transformed our lives! To have it captured in this book is a gift—it is like sitting across the dinner table from "Pastor Bo" and receiving great truth and wisdom from his decades of walking with God. Bo's life echoes what is written in these pages! We encourage you to read it with an open heart as you discover more of your identity as a new creation in Christ.

Daniel and Bree Proffitt
Pastors, Trinity Fellowship Church

I've had the privilege of serving alongside of Pastor Bo in the trenches of the local church for more than two decades. Bo stands out as a true pastor, seamlessly embodying the essence of the message he imparts. In tackling a frequently misconstrued subject, Bo has skillfully broken it down into an easily digestible format, making it accessible to all. His teaching style is characterized by grace and empowerment, truly reflecting a profound understanding of God's Word.

Matt Spears
Executive Pastor, Trinity Fellowship Church

The resonance of the word "Grace" is truly powerful, and Pastor Bo exemplifies it more than most. His profound embodiment of grace stems from a steadfast commitment to seek God and prioritize Him above all else. In this season, where such words are essential, Pastor Bo's gentle teaching style serves as a healing and comforting balm. Embrace the grace that permeates his teaching, allowing it to nurture and support you.

Amy E. Spears MA, LPC—S, NCC
Founder, LiveWell Counseling

NEW

Already *and* Becoming

B O   W I L L I A M S

 TrinityFellowship

Published in Amarillo, Texas, by Trinity Fellowship Church

Unless otherwise noted, all scripture translations are *The Holy Bible: New King James Version, Copyright* © 1982 by Thomas Nelson. Used by permission. All rights reserved.

Scripture quotations marked (NASB) are *New American Standard Bible,* Copyright © 2020 by the Lockman Foundation. Used by permission. All rights reserved.

Printed in the United States of America

ISBN Paperback: 978-1-7331281-2-4
ISBN Ebook: 978-1-7331281-3-1

CONTENTS

FOREWORD

I remember the day I got my first new car. We had purchased a couple of new vehicles for our family over the years, but this was *my* first new car—a shiny, black, four-door BMW 325i, BMW's entry-level car. I had longed to own a Bimmer. The day we drove it off the lot, I was so excited! The smell of new leather. The way it accelerated and handled corners. Even now, I can remember that feeling of freedom and pure joy.

No offense to our wonderful American car manufacturers, but the German engineers are obsessed with the driving experience. One of the unique things about BMW cars is their 50:50 weight balance. They go to extreme lengths to try and split the car's weight evenly between the front and rear axles. This makes for a great driving experience, as the car seems to turn around the driver. It's something I should have considered when I decided to turn off the Dynamic Traction Control on an icy road in December.

I had all three of my young children in the car with me. We were headed home, and the empty road was perfectly icy. I was going to be the "fun Dad" and demonstrate my driving skills with a few fishtails. I tried, but the traction control computer kept setting us straight. So, I turned it off. The next thing I knew, we were not fishtailing. We were doing 360s in the middle of the road! I have no idea how many times we rotated (it was many!). My kids thought it was the best thing ever as I yelled, "No, this is not supposed to be happening!"

Thank God he watches over the foolish! Our adventure came to a stop as we bumped into the curb facing the wrong way, having miraculously missed every parked car on the roadside. I quickly re-engaged traction control and tried, unsuccessfully, to convince the kids not to tell Mom.

My problem was that I learned how to drive in a pickup truck where all the weight was in the front. I did not know how to drive a BMW in these conditions. It was something completely new and foreign to me. It somehow "felt right," yet my ignorance got me into a situation where I was completely out of control.

Being "born again" is not unlike this experience. It is, of course, way more significant than getting a new car, but we still have to learn how to live in this new reality. As the Apostle Paul says in Ephesians 4:

> *But that is not the way you learned Christ! — assuming that you have heard about him and were taught in him, as the truth is in Jesus, to put off your old [man], which belongs to your former manner of life and is corrupt through deceitful desires, and to be renewed in the spirit of your minds, and to put on the new self, created after the likeness of God in true righteousness and holiness.*[1]

Scripture is clear. When we accept Christ as our Lord and savior—receiving his death as the price for our sin and believing he was raised from the dead, thereby proving he is the Son of God—we are born again as something completely new! To be successful in the Christian walk, we need to learn how to "drive" this new creation.

This can be especially challenging if you, like me, grew up in a religious persuasion that taught salvation was something slippery and uncertain, that you were going to be constantly at war with the "sin nature" inside of you, and that God was a scorekeeper tracking every good and bad deed and weighing us against the balance.

---

1 The Holy Bible, English Standard Version (Eph 4:20–24). (2016). Crossway Bibles

The Good News is that none of this is true! The Gospel of Christ is so much more powerful than we imagine. To fully understand what Jesus accomplished on the cross will take a lifetime of study and possibly all of eternity to process. But to get started, you are holding the perfect book in your hands!

I met Pastor Bo Williams over 30 years ago when Kim and I first started attending Trinity Fellowship Church. Over the years of serving together, he has become a dear friend, a trusted advisor, and a mentor. He has spent the past couple of decades studying the subject of the "new man," drawing deep from his personal experience and learning. Bo is truly an expert on this subject, and over the years, he has helped me greatly in my understanding of what Christ accomplished on the cross.

Bo is the epitome of the Ephesians 4 gift of pastor/teacher Christ presents to his church. His heart for discipling people has been demonstrated time and again as hundreds of individuals, me included, can attest to, and he has a deep passion for understanding and teaching scripture.

This book will take you on a journey to discover the power of the "new man" Christ made you to be, and instead of wrestling with your so-called "sin nature," you will learn how to lean into the relationship Christ offers us. You will find that the power of a relationship with God is so much greater than the power of sin that tries to hold you back. It is not willpower but the Holy Spirit's power that sets us free!

I encourage you to see this as a journey and not merely something to read. Jesus has something he wants to show you. He died to allow you to be something completely new. Let him show you the way.

Jimmy Witcher Senior Pastor
Trinity Fellowship Church
Author of Kingdom Come

INTRODUCTION

Many years ago, during a weekend Bible course on the book of James, I was confronted with a conundrum. Was the teacher correct? In the passage about faith without works being dead, he taught that the continuation of our salvation was contingent on the evidence of our faith through works and bearing fruit and victory over sin. Rosanne, my wife, pushed back, and though the format of the class provided for discussion and questions, it still created a moment of tension. Rosanne, to her credit, very simplistically defined her faith through her relationship with Christ—that it was real, that she was forgiven, and that she was very secure in her eternal destiny. The teacher turned to me and politely said, "You will need to help her with that at home, brother!"

But I had more confidence in Rosanne than the teacher. Of course, we did talk about it at home, and I loved where our conversation went. I know how real my relationship with Jesus is and Rosanne's is at least that real. She helped untie the knot that the teacher tied. But it would still be several more years before I would get the breakthrough in my understanding of scripture that would be life changing.

I believe the word *new* is on a short list of God's favorite words. The Greek word for *new* used most often is *kainos*, which means qualitatively new contrasted with numerically new. It is a word that means different, consecrated for new use, new living, new life, new being, new identity.

Jesus could not just exercise His will for things to be new. He had to make them new. He couldn't just make a good effort. He had to accomplish His finished work. He had to accomplish a new creation. *Therefore, if anyone is in Christ, he is a new creation; old things have passed away; behold, all things have become new.* 2 Corinthians 5:17

When you were born again, whether that was yesterday or thirty years ago, you were made new. You became a new creation. So, what happened to the old? Our old self died and was assigned to the tomb where it remains today—dead, buried, and without any power to influence you. But it is difficult for us to believe that, when we think of old thoughts and entertain old temptations and perhaps even commit old sins. You have probably been told many times that you have two natures that war within you. Sometimes the old nature wins, sometimes the new nature wins. Indeed, apart from Christ our life might not resemble Him at all.

But if I told you that the scripture teaches something very simply, clearly, and *"is the truth that sets you free"*[2] would you be open to hearing that? It could change your life. There is a battle, indeed, and we are called to a life of very active and resolute action. But it may not be what you think.

Do we need another book on grace? There have been some great ones in recent years and a search on the subject yields some older classics that are also very good. So, why another one?

Any Christian books that are written to help others either come to faith or to grow in their faith are needed. Regarding grace and our new identity in Christ, the more perspectives that are shared, the better. In my view, there is not a more important theological subject as it is the core and heartbeat of our relationship with Christ and the essence of our being. It is so important, in fact, that the enemy targets our understanding of grace and our identity more than any other. It was true in Paul's day when the New Testament was being written and it is true today. Though

2 John 8:32

Paul dealt with many doctrinal issues and subjects of the Christian life, his core subject was grace and our identity. Paul was compelled to do this because the religious establishment was a force to be reckoned with. The very dynamic of the conflicts over grace and works, freedom and performance, and guilt and righteousness has held the church hostage for two thousand years.

At this time in my life and faith journey, I felt compelled to write my personal story of discovery of the revelation of what I call *grace and the new man*. It is a great personal story of redemption, freedom, and victory and it's a story that fortunately affected many other people and, on some level, helped a very good church become even better.

I titled the book *New: Already and Becoming* because at salvation, we are made new but must grow up into our new identity. There are many biblical issues that will be unpacked along the way, hopefully answering some of your questions that have been some of mine. My understanding of grace and our identity is dynamic—it continues to develop as I continue to grow. I can see why some books have updated editions. I hope that when I read this one again in five years it still makes sense.

The book is divided into three sections, each with several short chapters. Each section has a purpose in mind. I urge you to read this book with an open mind and read all of it in order. Some chapters you may like more than others, but they all have purpose. But most of all, see what your Bible says about these issues and questions.

I have prayed this prayer of the Apostle Paul for everyone who reads this book, so I have prayed this for you! *That the God of our Lord Jesus Christ, the Father of glory, may give to you the spirit of wisdom and revelation in the knowledge of Him, the eyes of your understanding being enlightened; that you may know what is the hope of His calling, what are the riches of the glory of His inheritance in the saints, and what is the exceeding greatness of His power toward us who believe, according to the working of His mighty power which He worked in Christ when He raised Him from the dead and seated Him at His right hand in the heavenly places, far above all principality and power and might and dominion, and every name that is named, not only in this age but also in that which is to come. And He put all things under His feet, and gave Him to be head over all things to the church, which is His body, the fullness of Him who fills all in all.* Ephesians 1:17–23

Part 1

YOU ARE A NEW CREATION!

It was a new day! I knew I was different! Waking up the morning after my decision to surrender my life to Christ and being water baptized (the same day), was *the first day of the rest of my life.* That old expression has real meaning when it has real meaning! It was a good day. I couldn't articulate much about what happened, or how it happened, but it did happen, and I knew my life would never be the same.

Knowing something to be true is not the same thing as living that truth. My story will be told in bits and pieces throughout this book—the challenges, ins and outs, setbacks and victories. You have a story also. Everyone's story of their salvation and subsequent life is unique but similar in some respects. My hope and desire in the telling of my story and the lessons I have learned is to somehow help you.

Are you a sinner saved by grace, or a saint who sometimes sins? This question will circulate in the pages of this book multiple times as it is a major part of my personal story. I vividly remember the first time I not only stated this question to a group of men, but it was the first time I even considered such a choice of options. And as they found out that day, related to your identity in Christ, there is only one answer and there isn't a blend of the two options. You believe you are one or the other. One of the options is clearly the right one.

In this first of three sections I present the biblical picture of how you and I were given a completely new identity when we became a new creation in Christ.

Chapter 1
MY STORY

Do not marvel that I said to you, 'You must be born again.' The wind blows where it wishes, and you hear the sound of it, but cannot tell where it comes from and where it goes. So is everyone who is born of the Spirit."
—JOHN 3:7,8

Mr. Bayless offered me a job on the spot. I wasn't expecting that, and I stammered as I responded with "I don't really know if I want to go to Amarillo." You see, I had signed up for many interview opportunities as school districts visited the Eastern New Mexico University campus looking for teacher prospects. I figured that a shotgun approach would at least give me practice in interviewing.

My heart's desire was to move either to Sedona, Arizona where my best friend lived, or Roswell, New Mexico where I had many friends. But Amarillo? Texas? I had been there once but knew no one there, or anything about Amarillo—other than it was a small city in the Texas panhandle.

Mr. Bayless was the Assistant Superintendent for personnel for the Amarillo Independent School District. This interview was about half-way through the thirteen interviews I was scheduled for. I had phone interviews with the superintendents of Sedona and Roswell—both superintendents expressing interest but without knowing what vacancies they might have, there was no job offer. The other districts I had interviews with all seemed interested but gave the same response. So, I was very surprised to have an offer on the table from Amarillo in mid-April for the next school year. Mr. Bayless side stepped my uncertain response and encouraged me to make the two-hour drive to check out Amarillo—which I did two weeks later.

My visit to Amarillo and the school district was cordial and pleasant. I was shown to a couple of schools and saw some programs and met some people—all genuinely friendly. Mr. Bayless explained to me that if I accepted a position, I would be assigned to a school later in the summer. A contract awaited me in his office. I signed it, feeling a peace and security that I had a job for sure, but also with the thought that this would be for one year. After a year's experience, I reasoned, I would go somewhere I really wanted to go to. Out of the thirteen applications and interviews I participated in; I would later receive eleven offers including Sedona and Roswell! As a male teacher in elementary (rare in those days) and with a master's degree in the teaching of reading, I would be in bigger demand than I dreamed. But I had signed a contract and though I could have broken it, I had an internal value learned and modeled from my father to be a man of my word. Also, I would learn many times the truth of Proverbs 16:9—*The mind of man plans his way, But the LORD directs his steps.*

My steps were to be ordered by the Lord. In Amarillo, I would grow in my faith, meet my wife Rosanne, and be a part of a small group of people that would start a church named Trinity Fellowship, which would grow to be a significant church to the Amarillo community as well as to the world! That one-year commitment I made blew by me exceedingly fast. I was rooted to stay.

The year I moved to Amarillo and began teaching at Western Plateau Elementary School was 1976. I had been a Christian a little over four years, coming to faith the spring semester of my freshman year, on March 31, 1972—Easter Sunday.

I intentionally chose ENMU as my college destination for the number one reason that Portales was seven hours from Deming, New Mexico, my hometown. That was too far to be a weekend suitcase destination where I would be expected to go home on weekends. I wanted a little more adventure (but not too much), so I went where I knew only a few people. My thought was, "Let the adventure begin!" I was assigned to Eddy Hall dormitory, first floor north. Destiny! And I was hired for part-time work at Hatch Packing Company to work on the kill floor. Destiny? Not so much!

My upbringing in Deming was clean, interesting, uneventful, mostly safe, and innocent. On Interstate 10, north of the Mexican border town of Palomas, this small town of about 8000 was a town you passed through on your way west to California or east to Texas (El Paso, San Antonio, and Houston). Nestled in the Rio Mimbres farming valley and surrounded by desert mountains, it had a beauty of its own. It was known for its pure drinking water pumped from an underground aquifer before the advent of cheap bottled water and which today irrigates a significant amount of green chili grown in fertile fields. Hatch chili, grown nearby in Hatch New Mexico, is the same variety. I owe my highly developed palate for spicy New Mexican food to my mom's flat red enchiladas and to a few excellent restaurants in the region. Deming is also famous for the nearby Pancho Villa raid of Columbus, New Mexico—thirty miles to the south and just north of the Mexican border. The Junior High I attended was the tallest building in Deming and was used as a lookout for Villa.

Other than that, the pace was slow and uneventful. Deming could have passed as any typical American small town for a boy to grow up in the 50s and 60s. Crime was low, the streets were safe, and I could be gone all day playing with friends in any part of town without my parents knowing my whereabouts or being concerned. Transportation was by bicycle—you could be anywhere in town quickly. Neighborhood vacant lots were taken over by us to build bike trails and jumps—without knowing who the owners were. It didn't matter, no one cared. Weekends always included Saturday afternoon trips to the El Rancho theater for the week's new showing (35-cent admission left 10 cents for a soda and a 5-cent glazed donut at Dane's bakery after the show).

Sundays? My mom took us to church faithfully until I was about ten years old and then attendance fell off sharply. She did it mostly to please her parents. I have few memories—neither good nor bad—of those years of church attendance—other than it was boring. My Dad never attended, and this is an important part of the story—his life.

My Dad was an awesome man and was very highly respected and admired in his community. He was part owner and the manager of Deming Packing Co.—a small full-processing meat plant that mostly served the southern New Mexico communities as their primary source of meat and sausage products. D-PAC, as it was known, was the first plant to include mesquite wood along with hickory to smoke hams and bacon—ahead of its time! The business was moderately successful and was one of the town's largest employers. Dad's consistent generous treatment of his employees and his faithful community involvement earned him a reputation that he consistently lived up to. He was a good man. A very good man. From him, I would learn the truth of Proverbs 22:1—*A good name is to be more desired than great wealth; Favor is better than silver and gold.*

We were middle class, though we lived very modestly. I never experienced insecurity about where our next meal would come from, but we weren't spoiled. These are traits that, even today, are still wired into me and my brother and sister and are a part of my heritage that I treasure. The point of this is that I so admired my dad that I wanted to be like him. I noticed and paid attention to how he treated people and how people responded to him. I was proud of my dad. I knew enough of his life story to be especially proud.

He grew up in a very small community in northeastern New Mexico called Capulin. His dad, Oscar, was trying to eke out a living working hard at dryland farming on their homestead property. When Dad was about twelve, he and his four siblings left with their mother who filed for divorce, and they moved to Oklahoma City. Shortly after moving, Oscar died of cancer. A few years later, their mom died from complications from a botched surgery. So, at the age of fifteen, Dad was orphaned along with his two brothers and two sisters—during the depression! The kids were farmed out to various foster families and relatives, and Dad and his older brother lived with aunts until graduating from high school. Each of the five siblings would live very different and successful lives despite the adversity each faced. Some of it was due to family heritage and some was due to the values of the "Greatest Generation." They all made it.

What was lacking in the Williams heritage was religious faith. My mom was a believer but very quiet about her faith. My dad would come to describe himself as an agnostic—one who doesn't know whether there is a God or not or what to believe in, if anything. An agnostic is full of questions. He would explain to me later that he struggled with believing in the miraculous. Therefore, he couldn't believe in the authority of the Bible, though he admired Jesus and his teachings. But those explanations were never discussed in our home. He never discouraged our church attendance and never spoke negatively of religious faith. So, how did I process all that and what effect did it have on me?

During my high school years, I did as many high schoolers would do—I started dreaming about my future. I can say my ambitions for life were not about making money, owning businesses, or politics—but about living an honorable life that treated people well, like my dad. Spiritually, I was devoid of faith. I never would have articulated that I was an agnostic, but looking back, I was. My Dad didn't need faith. Why would I?

The summer after my senior year, I found myself at a Campus Crusade for Christ rally in a local park. One of the leaders who connected with me personally was a few years older and was someone I really respected. His pursuit of me inspired me and got my attention, though falling short of me making a decision for Christ. But the seed was planted and would be watered by many sources when I started my freshman year at ENMU.

Campus Crusade for Christ. Navigators. Various campus ministries—the Bible Chair, the Baptist Student Union, the Campus Christian House—all would water that seed. But most of all would be the friends I would make at Eddy Hall, first floor north. I had two groups of friends. The intellectual party group and the group of "Jesus Freaks," the born-again hippies who were relatively new believers, young in the faith, untrained in the Word, but completely sold out for their relationship with Jesus Christ. The "Jesus Movement" or "Jesus Revolution" was having an impact on most college campuses, including ENMU. It had an impact on me.

During the fall semester I lived like I wanted to—partying and carousing. I never got into the drug scene, but I liked drinking and girls and the party scene. But I also accepted invitations to go to Bible studies and devotionals. Most importantly, I accepted friendship overtures with the "Jesus Freaks". They weren't preachy or religious. But they were authentic, and I knew they cared about me.

Friendship with the party intellectual group was different. There were some good guys in that group, but values such as sincerity and generosity were lacking. One of them, the strongest of the intellectuals, loved to get into debates with the young Christians. He was a good debater and if the arguments had been scored by a debate judge, he would've won hands down. But the reality as I perceived it was that the Christians were the winners because their spirit was good, and their kindness prevailed. The friendships formed with the Christians were more authentic and more than surface deep.

As the year went on, I felt myself pulled between the two groups. God was working on my heart. So, in the spring of that year on Easter weekend, I went with my dorm roommate to his home near Albuquerque for the weekend. It was an uneventful weekend, and I was oblivious to the fact that it was Easter. But that Sunday afternoon as we traveled back to Portales, riding in Larry's car (a 1969 Dodge Challenger, a muscle car), I decided to surrender my life to Jesus! I prayed some kind of prayer in silence—what exactly I prayed I don't know. Larry was unaware of any of this. When I got back to the dorm, I rounded up some of the Jesus Freak friends and told them I wanted to be baptized. I didn't know language like "saved" or "born again"—but they knew what I meant and within thirty minutes we were at a local church and I was standing in the baptistry with two of my friends, Gary Jinks and Skip Forsythe.

Over fifty years ago I still vividly remember the experience. I was nervous—not about whether I was making the right decision, but because I knew my life would never be the same. The immersion into water that night I would later come to understand as an "all in" experience—I got all wet! My identity changed that day, beginning with my decision that afternoon and now being embodied that night through the obedient act of water baptism. I was stepping over a line into a new life and I would never come back to where I was. I knew almost nothing about the Bible or theology, but I knew my life was changing. All the seed planted in me by faithful people was germinating and growing. I knew three things—my sins were forgiven, I had a new Lord and Master, and God had a plan for my life. That night, that was all I knew but it was enough. My decision was a decision of my will. It was not an emotional decision though emotion was involved. It was a decision of my will and more than fifty years later it remains the decision that it was that day.

The morning after my baptism I woke up feeling different. I knew the big three—I was forgiven, I had a personal relationship with Jesus as Lord and Savior, and God had a plan for my life. And I had a zeal to tell others about my decision. As I began to learn the Word and walk out my faith, I would learn more about why I felt different. But it would be many years before I would get the personal revelation of how different I was. I would later learn that my first baptism was not in water, but a spiritual baptism of me into Christ, which I will explain soon.

There were immediate and significant changes in my life. I quit partying and didn't even have the desire to do so. I intentionally started using my beer money for a better cause, adopting an orphan from India for 12.00 a month. in 1972 you could buy a lot of beer with 12.00! I considered that adopting the orphan was a symbolic but significant change to remind myself that I was a new and different person. I cleaned up my language, became more diligent in my college studies, and started a regular daily routine that, for a college student, was quite conservative. Overall, I grew up quickly and became more responsible.

I wanted to be a difference-maker right away and began seeing people with different eyes. I became aware of their needs and struggles, and I had the desire to help them. I was always considered to be a nice person, but now I was very aware of who I was as Christ's ambassador.

Chapter 2

EARLY GROWTH

Then He spoke many things to them in parables, saying:
"Behold, a sower went out to sow. And as he sowed, some seed fell
by the wayside; and the birds came and devoured them. Some
fell on stony places, where they did not have much earth; and
they immediately sprang up because they had no depth of earth.
But when the sun was up they were scorched, and because they
had no root they withered away. And some fell among thorns,
and the thorns sprang up and choked them. But others fell on
good ground and yielded a crop: some a hundredfold, some
sixty, some thirty. He who has ears to hear, let him hear!"

MATTHEW 13: 3–9

M y salvation, or new birth as I would come to call it later, was in the spring of 1972, on Easter Sunday. I went home to Deming in May and told my grandparents about being baptized. Their denomination put a premium on baptism and after they were assured that I was baptized in the "correct church," they were pleased. I had always believed that my Granny prayed for me and shortly after hearing about my salvation/ baptism, she passed away from a stroke. I still believe my news was one of her final blessings this side of heaven.

That summer, there were two events linked together that were significant to my new faith. The first was my role in helping to lead Jock Whitworth, my best friend from high school to the Lord. I found out soon after coming home that Jock had been arrested for marijuana possession. He would later receive probation, but the incident rocked his world. I immediately shared with him about my conversion and his response over the next few days was to surrender his own life to Jesus. Though Jock and I attended different colleges, we spent the next four summers traveling together and every trip had a spiritual focus. We would pass out tracts, witness to people, attend various events and churches, and have adventure doing things in places like Yellowstone National Park, southern California, and Colorado.

In the summer of 1972, Jock and I attended Explo '72 in Dallas, Texas—a huge youth event that drew young people from all over the U.S. We caught a ride to El Paso where we boarded a bus to Dallas with a bunch of young people we didn't know. Host homes in Dallas housed the several hundred thousand youth who filled the city. The host home Jock and I stayed at was with a very nice family, members of a Methodist church, and they had teenagers who also attended the event. We were shuttled between main events at large outdoor gatherings and breakout events at local churches. Evening events were headlined by some of the new Christian music groups and nationally known speakers such as Bill Bright. Explo '72 was such a divinely provided experience for a new believer like me. It was a deep dive discipleship experience for me—the first of many great learning and growing experiences I would have. Since it was closely connected to the Jesus Revolution that was culminating about that time, it went a long way to bridge the gap between the movement and local churches.

My next significant period of growth took place during my sophomore year in college. ENMU was a state college, but they allowed Bible classes taught by certified instructors to be counted as electives credit.

So, I took three courses over the next three semesters—Old Testament Survey, New Testament Survey, and Philosophy of Religion. The two survey courses were especially helpful since they required reading the Old and New Testaments in their entirety. It was significant that within my first year as a believer that I read the Bible all the way through, along with getting classroom instruction from good teachers. Two outstanding results came from that experience—a first systematic exploration of the Scriptures, and the beginning of a love for the scriptures. Both results would bear fruit from then on.

In the spring semester of 1973, at about the one-year anniversary of my salvation, some of the original Jesus Freak friends would begin talking to me about a new experience they had encountered—something called the Baptism in the Holy Spirit. The timing of this for me was good. I felt in need of something that was new and fresh. I certainly wasn't in a spiritual crisis. I was steady, faithful, and diligent—but I felt like there was more. The answer to that was in seeking the Holy Spirit.

So, seek I did! Besides conversations with my friends, I had heard that one of the Bible Chair professors had also received the Baptism in the Holy Spirit. His name was Fount Shultz, and though he was only at the University for one more semester, Fount would make an important and much needed impression on me.

I read the book, "A New Song," by Pat Boone. Pat Boone was a talented singer of his generation, in the same genre of Frank Sinatra and Nat King Cole. So, my generation was aware of him, but we were still a generation removed. Someone gave me a copy of his book and his testimony was the perfect story for me. He was in a denomination that believed and taught a doctrine known as "cessationist doctrine," which says spiritual gifts ceased with the writing of the scriptures that later became the canon of the Bible. The doctrine states that these spiritual gifts were no longer needed to authenticate the ministry and message of the early Apostles.

I certainly was no Bible scholar, but that argument didn't seem right to me. Surely, I reasoned, there were other purposes and reasons for spiritual gifts that were needed by the church today. Pat Boone's story told of his inquiry into the Holy Spirit which led to searching and pursuing all God had for him, including being baptized in the Holy Spirit with subsequent results. I read the book, closed it, and said to the Lord—*"I want this. I want anything and everything you want me to have, and I want all of it. If there is something I need that will deepen my faith, strengthen my walk, and draw me closer to You—I want it."*

I said that as a prayer, and I believe at that moment I received what I was asking for. There was no accompanying emotion for me, just a belief that God gave me what I asked for. My prayer was based on Luke 11:9-13 (NASB)—*So I say to you, ask, and it will be given to you; seek, and you will find; knock, and it will be opened to you. For everyone who asks, receives; and he who seeks, finds; and to him who knocks, it will be opened. Now suppose one of you fathers is asked by his son for a fish; he will not give him a snake instead of a fish, will he? Or if he is asked for an egg, he will not give him a scorpion, will he? If you then, being evil, know how to give good gifts to your children, how much more will your heavenly Father give the Holy Spirit to those who ask Him?*

Two weeks later, I would seek help and prayer from Fount Schultz to receive my prayer language. The entire experience was a signature moment in my life that has been an important part of my continued growth from that day forward. It was then that I learned that my experience was part of a significant and growing movement that had been going on for several years called the Charismatic Renewal.

All was well for almost a year except for one thing—there was a serious flaw in our Christian community as it pertained to this new experience we were walking in. The flaw wasn't in the Baptism in the Holy Spirit or the spiritual gifts. It was because there were no seasoned, mature, wise leaders to guide and disciple us. Fount Schultz had moved on and as we looked around at each other, we were all newbies. Self-taught Christians are limited and vulnerable. Strong healthy churches have leadership in place that disciple new and young believers well. It is clearly taught in the book of Acts and the epistles that danger awaits opportunities to damage the sheep.

> *For I did not shrink from declaring to you the whole purpose of God. Be on guard for yourselves and for all the flock, among which the Holy Spirit has made you overseers, to shepherd the church of God which He purchased with His own blood. I know that after my departure savage wolves will come in among you, not sparing the flock; and from among your own selves men will arise, speaking perverse things, to draw away the disciples after them.* Acts 20:27-30

I would soon learn an important lesson that has served me well in future years of church leadership.

Chapter 3
OVERCOMING CRISIS

Therefore take heed to yourselves and to all the flock, among which the Holy Spirit has made you overseers, to shepherd the church of God which He purchased with His own blood. For I know this, that after my departure savage wolves will come in among you, not sparing the flock. Also from among yourselves men will rise up, speaking perverse things, to draw away the disciples after themselves.
ACTS 20:28–30

Sometime early in my junior year, my friends began telling me about a Sunday afternoon experience they were attending weekly. It was held at a farm outside Portales for about three hours beginning at 2:00 in the afternoon. The owner of the farm was a former Baptist preacher named Roy who had been baptized in the Holy Spirit and who no longer associated himself with the Baptists or any other church. He had started his own. Each Sunday afternoon, after the end of the service, his wife would lay out a big spread of great home cooking—just what a bunch of single college students needed!

At first, the worship, fellowship, and teaching were great! There was excitement, exuberance, and the flow of the Holy Spirit and spiritual gifts was unhindered. Roy was an effective communicator, and his teaching was deep. This was not basic biblical teaching as I was accustomed to.

He seemed to "unlock" some of the mysteries in the Bible. He was able to draw some radical insights out of ordinary stories and passages, especially in the Old Testament. I admitted to myself that I didn't really understand it, but along with everyone else, I wanted to and would nod my agreement with oohs and aahs to everything he was saying. I figured that one day I would cross that line of revelation and be on the same page as Roy—I just needed to be submitted and patient until that day came.

But eventually, I noticed a shift in Roy's comments that troubled me. Roy talked of love but would increasingly drop negative remarks about churches and denominations and church leaders in the community. Once I noticed this inconsistency, I began noticing it every time it happened, and the frequency grew. One Sunday I realized that one of the young married couples stopped attending. That bothered me. They were friends of mine and I trusted them, so I went to talk to them. They simply said they felt something was off, but they weren't sure exactly what.

Soon after, I made the decision to quit attending, myself. This would begin the most difficult year of my Christian life. The decision itself wasn't all that difficult—my uneasiness was reason enough. But all my faith community was at Roy's farm. So, I found myself alone and disillusioned with really no one to talk to. This was my junior year of college and in terms of spiritual life, I had very little joy and peace. My year was one of solitude and loneliness—not what God intends for any of us. But it was also a year of growing in diligence. The spiritual disciplines of reading my Bible every day and praying saw me through this time of wilderness. I learned the value of strong personal commitment and of something I advise many young people, "stay the course!" And I of course learned the value of what I was missing the most—Christian community. I started attending local denominational churches for the two remaining years of my time in Portales.

I would later come to understand that I was in a toxic and dangerous situation at Roy's farm. It was typical of what happens when a cult leader with a strong fatherly personality takes captive young people who are especially susceptible. I also learned that his teaching was an aberrant form of ends time teaching known as "manifested sons of God," which taught that elite groups like Roy's would become "manifested sons," glorified Christ-like believers, supernaturally endowed to help the rest of the church through the tribulation. It would only be those who heard and believed the message from a prophet like Roy that would become manifested sons.

Eventually, that group would fall apart and unfortunately, most of those who stayed in the group became disillusioned with their faith and wandered away. I don't know the long-term outcome for any of them. How important is the charge Paul gave to Timothy—*"O Timothy, guard what was committed to your trust, avoiding the profane and idle babblings and contradictions of what is falsely called knowledge, by professing it, some have strayed concerning the faith. Grace be with you. Amen."*

Wilderness times are never fun. But when we press into our relationship with the Lord, they can be invaluable. In the wilderness, we learn a lot about ourselves and about God. We are strengthened and become wiser. We grow our capacity for wisdom and courage and become better able to help others. My senior and graduate years at ENMU were healthy and fruitful and fun. I survived that wilderness excursion and though there have been many since and more ahead, I no longer dread wilderness times. I embrace them in obedience.

Graduating from ENMU and taking that first job in Amarillo at Western Plateau Elementary School would be the next step toward my destiny. When I moved to Amarillo, I didn't know anyone. But a connection I had made while at ENMU would at least give me a name of a church to visit. So, I didn't shop around but joined the first and only church I attended when I arrived in Amarillo—Paramount Terrace Christian Church. Within a week I officially became a member, being very impressed overall with the church and especially the senior minister, a different Roy, Roy Wheeler. Though I differed doctrinally with the views of the church on the Holy Spirit, it was a great church for me to be a part of for the next two years. I was active, teaching Sunday School and helping to lead the college ministry. Roy Wheeler taught me the value of connecting with people as a leader. It was a healthy, growing church that gave me a good church experience. There I would meet other believers who were like minded about the Holy Spirit and through a series of events, we made a quiet, clean disconnect with Roy Wheeler's blessing to start a new church in Amarillo—Trinity Fellowship.

My involvement, along with my wife Rosanne's, in a pioneering work of starting a church was a fantastic experience. We joined with likeminded people who were surrendered to everything God had for us. The current mission statement of Trinity Fellowship is, *"To those hungry for an extraordinary life, Trinity Fellowship Church is a healthy family pursuing God, growing stronger, and impacting the world."* Though at the beginning we didn't have a mission statement, this one would have fit well. We were hungry and in pursuit of God. We didn't have a preaching pastor for over a year. If you wanted to preach or lead worship, you signed up. Sometimes it was ok, sometimes not so good. But when people visited, most of them stayed because there was a such passion for God!

Trinity also was very committed to the integrity and authority of scripture while being fully surrendered to the ministry and work of the Holy Spirit. We learned a lot in our early years and went over some big bumps in the road, but Trinity would become a large and influential church in the community that found expression and impact far outside of Amarillo. The story of the beginning of Trinity Fellowship and its forty-six-year history at the date of this writing would be a book of its own. It has been a joy to be a part of this amazing church!

My decision to move to Amarillo for one year was forgotten and put aside. People don't move to Amarillo for the climate or natural beauty. Amarillo's greatest asset is the people. I fell in love with the people—both where I worked and where I worshipped. But as my story continued, I continued to grow spiritually as the church grew, and as my career in education grew—everything grew together. Life was good!

Almost at the exact time we started Trinity Fellowship, I met Rosanne Galloway—a beautiful young lady both inside and out who was fanatically in love with Jesus. She was smart, strong, and very focused on her relationship with the Lord. The most attractive thing about her was her spiritual depth and discipline. Neither of us had any question at all that God brought us together. We were married six months later—the first wedding at Trinity. Over the next several years, we would have four wonderful children—two sons and two daughters. My two sons and a daughter are educators in public schools. All four are believers with families of their own. My favorite age of parenting is the one we are in now. Our children love being together as a family. What a blessing to see them love each other and live and enjoy life together as they do!

After twenty years, my career in the Amarillo Public Schools ended as I accepted a pastoral position on staff at Trinity. My decision to go into full time ministry was not "answering a call" as you sometimes hear the expression. I believed that my twenty years in public education were ministry. That is the way we should all believe about our vocational callings, or wherever we find ourselves. We are all in "full time ministry" all the time. But I was certain about my decision to make the change. As circumstances would have it, I had to wait nine months after the decision to make the change. I compared it to a pregnancy. I was pregnant with the new thing God was birthing in my life. About halfway through the pregnancy, I went through a big test. I was presented with an opportunity to stay in the school system with a significant advancement. I declined and knew it was the right decision. To me it felt a little like the testing Jesus went through in the wilderness.

At the time I joined the staff, Trinity was beginning a new ministry training endeavor. Already a large church and without a seminary or Bible college in the area, there was a need for good formal training of pastors and other church leaders. Trinity had started an association of churches called TFAC (Trinity Fellowship Association of Churches) many years before and many of the TFAC churches were asking for training resources. For the next eight years, we became a campus for Christian Life School of Theology, based in Columbus, Georgia. The format of CLST classes was monthly intensives taught over a weekend, ending with an exam and course credit for those seeking degrees. We had ten courses a year for the next eight years. Though the college was not accredited, the teaching was excellent. Faculty came from all over the U.S. from churches and institutions. Of the eighty courses offered from CLST, I would take seventy-nine of them and would become a faculty member for CLST—allowing me to teach at church campuses around the nation. These years would be some of the best years of my personal spiritual growth.

But despite the excellent biblical training and the health of Trinity Fellowship, there was still something missing in my biblical and spiritual grid I was unaware of.

Our Senior Pastor, Jimmy Evans, had a good friend in ministry named Clark Whitten. Clark pastored churches in Roswell, New Mexico, Oklahoma City, and Orlando. At least once a year, Jimmy would invite Clark to come speak. Clark always spoke on the same subject—grace. Whenever Clark would speak, you left feeling a certain way. You felt good, you felt hopeful, you felt clean, and you were glad Clark was there, and you wanted Clark to come back again. And he would. Time after time, after time. I would ask myself why I felt different after his messages? This led to a major, life-changing spiritual breakthrough. It was still a few years away, but God was doing a work of preparation in my heart, plowing some soil for some new seed—new to me.

At this point I had been a Christian for about thirty-five years and in ministry ten years. I had served in various capacities through some easy and good times and through some difficult and challenging times.

But the core event in telling all this story is to tell you of a major spiritual encounter that unfolded over a several month period that deeply affected me and everything in my life. I wasn't looking for a breakthrough and wouldn't have known I needed one. But God did, and Clark Whitten was but one of the people and events that God used to shake my world.

Chapter 4
SINNER OR SAINT?

To the church of God which is at Corinth, to those who are sanctified in Christ Jesus, called to be saints, with all who in every place call on the name of Jesus Christ our Lord, both theirs and ours: Grace to you and peace from God our Father and the Lord Jesus Christ.
1 CORINTHIANS 1:2,3

My men's life group had been going for about ten years. It was August 2006, and I was having lunch with Royce Gooch and Michael Dyer, both co-leaders for the group. Royce asked what our study was going to be when we started back up for the fall semester, a couple of weeks away. This men's group was a Bible study focus group. The goal was always to dive into the word and study and learn together and grow in our faith by becoming more biblically literate. We had been through a lot of different biblical topics and had studied different books of the Bible over the years. The men who came to this group loved the studies and they loved the Word. They wanted to learn. They were hungry.

I didn't know how to answer Royce's question about the topic because I didn't know what to call it. So, I began telling Royce and Michael about my recent spiritual journey of discovering new insight into Grace. I told them that God had been stirring some new things in me that summer and I was excited to explore a new and deeper understanding about who we really are in Christ. Then I pulled out a copy of *"Birthright,"* by David Needham, explaining that it was a book that was opening some new understanding that I was really excited about. Before I could finish my statement, Michael said that he had read that book and that every Christian should read it!

This all started for me about four months prior. A member of this life group and a close friend, John Ingerson, told me in a conversation that a chronic disease diagnosis he had been given in years previous was a real struggle for him. He believed the disease had a spiritual origin and not a natural one. He requested to go through deliverance ministry to deal with it. Though I had a lot of experience with deliverance ministry with Trinity's Freedom Ministry, I felt his request should be handled by someone with more experience than me. I suggested he contact a pastor in Hereford by the name of Dorman Duggan who had been doing deliverance ministry for many years. I didn't know Dorman personally, but I trusted his reputation.

Within a couple of weeks, John had made contact with Dorman and went to Hereford to spend a part of the day with him. The following week I asked John how it went. He said it went very well, but he was still trying to get his head wrapped around the experience. I continued to ask questions—"What did he say? What did he do? Did he do any actual deliverance? Is there any change in your condition?"

John said that Dorman prayed for him, but he mostly just talked and quoted scripture. I pressed for more information out of curiosity. He didn't or couldn't give me a clear answer because it was so new to him, but he said that he believed Dorman was on to something. And then he told me Dorman wanted to meet me. I remember being a little disappointed as I was looking for results for John's original purpose in having the meeting. But a few weeks later I called Dorman anyway and drove to Hereford to meet him for lunch.

Dorman was a super nice guy and eager to talk with me. It wasn't a conversation as much as it was just listening to Dorman talk. I did make a couple of statements and ask a few questions. But really, it was just Dorman giving a lengthy and detailed treatise about what he believed happened at salvation, and he supported it with a lot of scripture. He hardly took a breath or stopped to eat his lunch. He was full of excitement, joy, and passion on a level I had seldom seen, and that exceeded my own. It was like he had something or knew something I didn't have. Even so, I had serious misgivings about what he was saying. It sounded too good to be true. My own study of the Bible was thorough, and I just differed with some of his conclusions.

My primary objection was that, though it sounded great, it just didn't line up with people's life experiences. I asked him, "If this is true, then why do people still struggle? And fail?" As I drove back to Amarillo, I remember shaking my head and thinking, "Dorman just can't be right." But I didn't shake it. I couldn't shake it. I couldn't get it out of my head.

In my bookcases at home were dozens of books I hadn't read. I'm a reader. One time, I took the Strengths Finder test, which gives you your top five strengths out of thirty-four. Three of my top five had to do with study and learning. I'm just wired this way—having an insatiable appetite to learn and know and understand new things. I always have at least two books I'm reading and sometimes three of four. About a week after my lunch with Dorman, I went to my bookcase to pick my next book, and what caught my eye was the book *Birthright*, by David Needham. It was a used book that I picked up out of a box of discarded books and that had been sitting on my shelf for a few years. But that was the book that I selected to read. I now believe the Holy Spirit set my eyes on that book out of the many to choose from. I read it. *Birthright* said the same thing as Dorman, in slightly different words. Wow! Now the Lord had my attention.

After *Birthright*, I listened to a teaching on CD by the teacher Graham Cook. *It said the same thing.* Mid-summer, I went to an Andrew

Wommack conference in Colorado Springs. The conference was on a different topic, but while there I picked up a few of his books. I read *Body, Soul, and Spirit,*—*it said the same thing.* I read David Needham's book again. I also remembered a book I had read years before, Neil Anderson's *Victory Over the Darkness*, about the power of knowing the truth about our identity in Christ—*the same basic thing.* Now, I was in a conundrum. Something was stirring in me that I believed was the Teacher inside of me (the Holy Spirit), but I was resisting completely giving in. I just had too many questions. Something wasn't adding up. Then I remembered something from seven months earlier.

At the beginning of every year, Trinity has an event called Zion. It was what some churches would call revival, but we called it Zion. It is a special, beginning of year time to consecrate ourselves to God for the coming year, seek Him in a deeper way, and hear His voice for our church but also on a personal level for ourselves. Zion always encourages fasting of different kinds including our diet but also media and anything that would distract us from hearing God. We were to be quiet before the Lord and subdue our flesh so that our spirit could be fed. And during Zion that year I believed the Lord spoke to me personally that I would encounter a new teacher or new teaching. It was vague, and I had all but forgotten it, but by the beginning of August, when I was in the midst of the whirlwind of the books I was reading and the teachings I was hearing, I remembered that prophetic voice that was directed at me. Now, I was getting excited!

As the discussion with Royce and Michael continued at lunch that day, we decided to call our new study, "Grace and the New Man." I didn't know what course it would take, and I had many questions and blank spaces in my understanding, but I was also very excited because I knew this was a God-breathed new adventure. I knew that as we studied it together, we would discover together. I was also encouraged that Michael was further down the road in his understanding. We would need his help.

At the end of August, we had our first life group meeting (we met on Thursdays at noon) in a room in our Children's Ministry building. Michael and Royce were there. John Ingerson was there, along with about twelve other guys, all sitting in a rectangular arrangement around tables. I began the meeting with a question that is a historic marker in our church. Every man there remembers it the same way and points to it as a defining moment in time. I asked the question, *"Are you a sinner saved by grace, or are you a saint who sometimes sins?"*

We went around the room so that each man could respond, and I had to clarify more than once that you couldn't choose both options—you had to choose only one. There were lots of comments and some questions, none of which went very deep that day. We stayed focused on the question of the day—*which are you?* The consensus answer of the group at the end of the meeting was that we were *saints who sometimes sin*, though why that was the right answer no one could really articulate. Those who were there will never forget that meeting. It started us on a quest for truth about our identity that would last for several years.

Chapter 5
READING THE BIBLE
AS IF FOR THE FIRST TIME

Therefore, if anyone is in Christ, he is a new creation;
old things have passed away; behold, all things have become new.
2 CORINTHIANS 5:17

The excitement of our new study was shared by everyone in the group, I think without exception. So, the group grew. For a group meeting at noon for a bunch of working men giving up their lunch, it became a big deal. You didn't want to miss a week. That group would grow from a dozen to thirty or more regular attendees. The original men in the group kept inviting friends. Word was getting around. There was something different being talked about every week and it was life giving.

I became intense in my devotion to studying to prepare for each week. I made outlines for us to follow and though I taught the material each week, it was the discussion that was the best part of the meetings. I welcomed the men to "push back" with their questions and challenges, which is very important. This study went on for years and we would wrestle together with questions and old beliefs until we could push through with a new understanding. The biblical picture of new wine in old wineskins was happening before our eyes. We had to freshen our wineskins in order for the Holy Spirit to fill us and teach us.

What about my study? Two things would have the biggest impact on me. The first was the most important—diving into the scriptures looking for the grace and new man message. I re-read the scriptures over and over, looking for it and finding it everywhere. *It was as though I was reading the Bible for the first time, it was so fresh!* Some people might object to the way I told this to our group, but I encouraged them to read the Bible looking for themselves in the scriptures. Of course, you will see Jesus everywhere, but you are everywhere also! And what is it the Word of God wants you to know about yourself? As I read scriptures that were very familiar to me, especially in the New Testament epistles, it was as though I was reading the Bible for the first time. The scriptures were fresh with understanding and depth and clarity. At the risk of sounding dramatic, it really was like a religious veil had been lifted.

Sinners or saints? That was a question I needed to know more about. I had not given that much thought or importance to identity up to this point. It wasn't that I didn't think it was important—I underestimated how much of a problem it is for so many Christians. And why is it so difficult? If the enemy can confuse us about the truth of who we are, we can never rise up to live in the truth of our identity. Grace is a target for the enemy, and religion is his domain. That sounds strong, but it is the very truth.

So, I went looking for the answer to that identity question. Almost all uses of "sinner" refer to people who are not born again; they are pre-faith people who need a savior. There are only a couple uses of the word that are arguably about believers—but maybe not! Paul referred to himself (1 Timothy 1:15) as the chief of all sinners, but it can easily be interpreted that he was referring to himself in that past tense time in his life when he persecuted the church. The other instance is James (4:8) exhortation to "cleanse your hands you sinners; and purify your hearts you double minded," the context of which could be salvation.

What about being called saints? An informal count using a

concordance, just in the epistles, gives us fifty-eight references where we are called saints. In every context imaginable we are called saints. If God has given us a new identity, which we will see in future chapters, has He given us a new name also? A great example I love to use is Paul's description of the leaders and members of the church at Corinth. Hear what he says about them when he identifies who they are:

> To the church of God which is at Corinth, to those who are sanctified in Christ Jesus, **called to be saints**, with all who in every place call on the name of Jesus Christ our Lord, both theirs and ours: Grace to you and peace from God our Father and the Lord Jesus Christ. 1 Corinthians 1:2,3

His description of them continues...

> I thank my God always concerning you for **the grace of God which was given to you by Christ Jesus, that you were enriched in everything by Him in all utterance and all knowledge,** even as **the testimony of Christ was confirmed in you,** so that **you come short in no gift,** eagerly waiting for the revelation of our Lord Jesus Christ, **who will also confirm you to the end, that you may be blameless** in the day of our Lord Jesus Christ. **God is faithful, by whom you were called into the fellowship of His Son, Jesus Christ our Lord.** 1 Corinthians 1:4-9

Do you remember what most of the content of the rest of the letter is about? Strong rebuke and correction for many issues, including factions and divisions and sexual immorality and scandalous partaking of the Lord's Supper, etc., etc. When you read about their problems, you wonder if any of them were even saved! I can imagine Paul, knowing how strong his correction and rebuke would be, realized that he needed to remind them of WHO they were first. Not only did their behavior not change their identity, but their identity revealed how abnormal their behavior was. So it is with us many times!

In my personal study and in the group discussions, there were problems that needed to be addressed and challenged and solved. Some of the old wineskin beliefs some of us had were an issue. I challenged myself to solve some of these scriptural issues. My belief in the authority of scripture and my ultimate and absolute respect for the scriptures would not allow anything other than an in-depth effort to figure these things out. In fact, I intentionally opened myself to the Holy Spirit and to the scriptures concerning any area of long-held doctrine I had. I wasn't a trained theologian—just a believer who loved Jesus and who loved and respected the authority of scripture.

THE ONE THING

My study and preparation continued and the discussion among the men in the group would bear fruit every week. There were times I struggled but we all struggled together. It was awesome! Then, I had a second significant study experience that would give me a breakthrough about the *one thing* that would untie the knot of my biggest misunderstanding about my identity in Christ.

This *one thing* has been taught in some circles all through church history, though it went largely missing at some point when church leadership and doctrine shifted more toward performance. Different movements through church history have had both positive and negative effects. The Holiness and Pentecostal movements in the latter part of the 19th and early part of the 20th centuries definitely moved the church toward performance. I realized that I was not only trapped in a performance issue with God, but I was helping others getting trapped.

Watchman Nee was a pastor in China in the early to mid—1900's. He has a long list of books under his name, many of which I've read. But one day I went to the same bookcase that gave me the book, *Birthright,* and pulled off a copy of Watchman Nee's book called, *The Normal Christian*

Life. I realized I had never read it, but again, the Holy Spirit pointed it out to me and reading it would unlock the most important part of my grace journey. To date, I have read and re-read this book seven or eight times—I've lost count. My original copy is so marked up and tattered I don't know if it will make it through another reading. It has been my delight to use this book as a study in small groups. There are many tremendous insights in this book about a lot of topics, but there was *one thing* that gave me a huge, "Aha!" moment in my journey. I call it *"The One Thing"* (clever, right?) When this domino fell, many dominoes fell. *What was the one thing?*

I was trying to understand my life in Christ without understanding my death in Christ. What God raises to new life has to first die. I'm not referring to daily dying to self that we speak of. I'm referring to something much more significant. There is something so clearly taught in the scriptures in plain sight that I had not seen, but Nee spoke of it with simple clarity. And when I saw it, I started seeing it everywhere.

Before I could be raised up with Christ to share in His resurrection life, I had to die with Him, or rather, in Him. *I have been crucified with Christ; it is no longer I who live, but Christ lives in me; and the life which I now live in the flesh I live by faith in the Son of God, who loved me and gave Himself for me.* Galatians 2:20

Who died? What died? And Why? Nee's book answered these questions, primarily using the text from Romans Chapter 6:

> *Or do you not know that as many of us as* **were baptized into Christ Jesus were baptized into His death?** *Therefore we were buried with Him through baptism into death, that just as Christ was raised from the dead by the glory of the Father, even so we also should walk in newness of life.* Romans 6:3,4

I had been taught in my early years as a believer that Romans 6 teaches us about water baptism—what it is and why it is so important. So, any time I read Romans 6, I naturally thought about water baptism and my frame of reference was my own water baptism. I now believe it is the opposite—*water baptism teaches us about Romans 6!*

In this very important biblical text, who died? I DID! How did I die? Through baptism into Jesus's death by crucifixion. Why did I die? The answer is in the following verses:

> *For if we have been united together in the likeness of His death, certainly we also shall be in the likeness of His resurrection, knowing this, that our old man was crucified with Him, that the body of sin might be done away with, that we should no longer be slaves of sin. For he who has died has been freed from sin.* Romans 6:5-7

Two clear answers are given to the why—First, for me to *live His life*, the resurrection life, I had to *die His death*. Second, the *who* that died was *my old man*—who I was in Adam. We are only looking at the first layer of the onion here. As we unfold this, there is more. But we first MUST know that we have died in Him and that before we can live in Him, we must recognize our death in Him. We are not simply identifying with Him. This is not just a metaphor or a symbolic expression. The wording Paul uses is definite and actual. How do we know that? Paul asks and answers an important question:

> *What shall we say then? Shall we continue in sin that grace may abound? Certainly not! How shall we who died to sin live any longer in it?* Romans 6:1-2

Something happened that I was unaware of on that Sunday afternoon in 1972 when I gave my life to Jesus in Larry Howell's car. In God's mercy, the first thing He did for me He did to me. He killed my old nature in Adam. That sounds too graphic. He did away with Bo's old self through death. Yes, He forgave me of my sins. But He did away with my body of sin. As Watchman Nee would explain, there is a difference in meaning between *sin* singular and *sins* plural. Sin, in the first five chapters of Romans, is a condition of the human race we inherited from Adam. We were born into it. Because we are born into Adam at birth, we are in the old creation corrupted by sin. As long as we are in Adam, that is whose nature we have. The only way out of Adam is through death. And not just any death—Jesus's death.

Sins are the individual acts I have committed that must be forgiven through His atoning work by His shed blood. But sin is something I must be delivered from, which I experience through baptism into His death. He shed his blood for my forgiveness. He gave His life for my deliverance. I had **two needs** that I could not remedy—forgiveness for what I had done (past, present, and future); and deliverance from who I was.

The picture in Romans 6 of this incredible act of God's grace and power and love is through baptism and union. *Baptizo* means immersion—all in! and through baptism into Christ, I have become united with Him—made in union with Him. As L. E. Maxwell describes it, it is not an imitation of Christ, it is a participation of and in Christ.

What follows death? What did they do with Jesus's body? It was buried. It was put in a tomb. What happened to my old nature? It was buried with Him. Is it still in the grave? Yes! So, who am I now? I am a new creation in Him. I am sharing in and living His resurrection life. Galatians 2:20, *It is no longer I who live, but Christ lives in me.*

The identity implications are enormous. I am not a sinner trying to become holy. I am a saint made holy by a new nature who is becoming aware of who I am and learning to live that new life in that holiness. I have been saved by radical grace—by His love and mercy and goodness and by His finished work on the cross that left nothing undone for me to have a new nature and a new life. When I was saved, God did not dust me off to make me clean so He could set me down to try again. He made me an altogether new person in Him! The life that I now live is His life. I'm living above sin by legally accessing from the supernatural heavenly realm the resurrected life.

If I get this wrong and believe that I am by nature who I always was, a sinner, then I am destined to continue in sin and fail. If all that has changed is that I have forgiveness, but that I am in essence who I have always been, then Romans 6 makes absolutely no sense, but Romans 7 does! I will inevitably fail. No, the genius of God is to make me a new person. Again, I am not a new person because I live differently, I live differently because I am a new person! My mind is being renewed to what is already a reality in my spirit. There is still a battle, but I'm fighting from a position of victory, not trying to get to one!

What is still in the future is my physical body, which has not been resurrected yet. His resurrected body is the first fruits of what is to come. My resurrected body—and yours—is what all creation groans and waits for. Paul writes of the future resurrection of our new bodies. But in the following passage on resurrection, the topic is much bigger than our future resurrected body. In these scriptures we see something we call the *divide of the cross*. Adam is of the old creation, as we were when we belonged to him. But Jesus is declared to be the second man and the last Adam. He is the beginning of a new humanity. All those who have passed through the cross have come to be a part of the new creation! We were image bearers of Adam—now we are image bearers of Christ!

> So also is the resurrection of the dead. The body is sown in corruption; it is raised in incorruption. It is sown in dishonor, it is raised in glory. It is sown in weakness, it is raised In power. It is sown a natural body, it is raised a spiritual body. There is a natural body, and there is a spiritual body. And so it is written, "**The first man Adam** became a living being." **The last Adam** became a life-giving spirit. However, the spiritual is not first, but the natural, and afterward the spiritual. **The first man was of the earth**, made of dust; **the second Man is the Lord from heaven**. As was the man of dust, so also are those who are made of dust; and as is the

heavenly Man, so also are those who are heavenly. And as we have borne the image of the man of dust, we shall also bear the image of the heavenly Man. 1 Corinthians 15:42–49

The one thing I did not know was that my old self was dead and buried and the new me is all that is alive. Once again, we revisit the glorious truth from Galatians 2:20 - *I have been crucified with Christ; it is no longer I who live, but Christ lives in me; and the life which I now live in the flesh I live by faith in the Son of God, who loved me and gave Himself for me.*

This is good news! Thanks be to God for this indescribable gift!

Chapter 6
SONSHIP

For as many as are led by the Spirit of God, these are sons of God.
For you did not receive the spirit of bondage again to fear, but you
received the Spirit of adoption by whom we cry out, "Abba, Father."
ROMANS 8:14,15

When I was 16, I bought by first vehicle—a 1966 Chevy pickup with a straight six engine block that got poor gas mileage. But I didn't care about mileage—all I cared about as a teenager was driving my truck. Gas was only 30 cents a gallon and I had a good paying job—1.25 an hour! I almost never had enough money to "fill it up," so I would pull into Mr. Clines gas station and put one or two dollars' worth of gas at a time in my pickup. One day Mr. Cline asked me why I didn't fill it up. After explaining my cash flow situation, he called me into his tiny office and showed me a card file box. He put my name at the top of a card and told me to write down what I couldn't pay and that I could pay the balance later. It was a type of credit card! When he saw the amazed look on my face that I would be trusted with such a transaction, he said—"Don't worry, I know who your father is!" That was the day I learned what it meant to be Skeeter's son! *A good name is to be more desired than silver and gold.*

The Bible uses pictures to help us see truths. After all, most of us are visual learners. But a picture that confused me was whether we are born again or adopted. Are we 'born again" as Jesus told Nicodemus we must be and as Peter wrote in his first epistle? Or are we adopted, as Paul said in Galatians 4:4-6, Romans 8:14-17, and Ephesians 1:5? Why didn't Paul speak of being born again? First, here are the scriptures referring to being *born again:*

> *Jesus answered and said to him, "Most assuredly, I say to you, unless one is **born again**, he cannot see the kingdom of God."* John 3:3

> *Blessed be the God and Father of our Lord Jesus Christ, who according to His great mercy has caused us to be **born again** to a living hope through the resurrection of Jesus Christ from the dead,* 1 Peter 1:3 (NASB*)*

> *Having been **born again**, not of corruptible seed but incorruptible, through the word of God which lives and abides forever,* 1 Peter 1:23

Now, the scriptures for *our adoption as sons:*

> *But when the fullness of the time had come, God sent forth His Son, born of a woman, born under the law, to redeem those who were under the law, that we might receive the **adoption as sons**. And because you are sons, God has sent forth the Spirit of His Son into your hearts, crying out, "Abba, Father!"* Galatians 4:4–6

> *For as many as are led by the Spirit of God, these are sons of God. For you did not receive the spirit of bondage again to fear, but you received the **Spirit of adoption** by whom we cry out, "Abba, Father." The Spirit Himself bears witness with our spirit that we are children of God, and if children, then heirs—heirs of God and joint heirs with Christ, if indeed we suffer with Him, that we may also be glorified together.* Romans 8:14–17

*Just as He chose us in Him before the foundation of the world, that we should be holy and without blame before Him in love, having predestined us to **adoption as sons** by Jesus Christ to Himself, according to the good pleasure of His will...*Ephesians 1:4–5

Paul or Jesus? Who was correct? The Sunday School answer, of course, would be Jesus—unless they both were. Paul is using a metaphor to describe *sonship by adoption* that functioned in the Roman legal system and since Gentiles were a primary audience for his writing, he often used metaphors meaningful to them. As they read or heard this metaphor, they would have known exactly what he was saying.

Roman adoption was a well-known legal practice in the Gentile world—not so in the Jewish world. In Jewish family life, when a child was orphaned, they were cared for by extended family members in most cases. But in Roman culture, adoption was very important—similar in some ways to how we would understand adoption, but unique in other ways. In the book, *"Paul's Metaphors,"* by David Williams [3], the process of Roman adoption is fascinatingly explained. The following is my rendition with a little liberty I take to better explain the concept.

As in many cultures, it was very important for a Roman head of household to have a son as an heir. Each family had their own household religion, and the head of the home was the family priest. An heir would perpetuate the priesthood, but of course would also perpetuate the name, the business, the heritage, and all those things of importance that needed to go into perpetuity.

The head of a Roman family was known as the *Pater Familia*—the head of the family. There could only be one *Pater Familia*, and his authority would extend over married sons who had their own households. The authority a son would have over his own household was called *patria potesta,* which was subservient to the *Pater Familia*.

---

3 Williams, David J. (1999). *Paul's Metaphors—Their Context and Character,* Hedrickson

This is more easily understood when we recall the movie, "*The Godfather.*" Don Corleone was the *Pater Familia*. He had three sons—Fredo, the oldest, Sonny, the middle son and the likely heir, and Michael, the youngest and the military hero who was outside the circle by his own choice.

Fredo didn't have the ability to succeed his father as head of the family. He would have a place in the family, but in a lesser role. Sonny had the ability and the commitment and the desire to ascend, but he had a serious flaw—a very bad temper. Michael was very capable but had no interest in the family business. Sonny is killed because of his temper and Michael has a change of heart and enters the family business and becomes the head of the family after the Godfather, *Don Corleone*, dies of a heart attack. That is the basic storyline, and it worked so well they made several sequels.

So, in Roman times, the head of a family didn't just need a son to be heir, he needed a capable son. Not a Fredo, but a Michael. Let's assume that a given family has no sons or only a Fredo. Where does he get a son to be heir? Through adoption. He could adopt a very capable household slave if he had one, but let's assume that he must look elsewhere. There is no adoption agency, and he is not interested in adopting an infant or a young boy. No, he needs to adopt an adolescent male—someone grown or almost grown that is known as very capable with a lot of potential.

We are making lots of assumptions, but let's build our story as we go because this is basically how adoption happened in Roman times. The man in our story (let's give him the name Paulus) notices a family that lives around the block who had an adolescent son. He is handsome, physically fit, intelligent, talented, and seems very capable. Paulus inquires around the neighborhoods and finds out more about this young man (let's give him the name Timotheus). He watches him and takes his time to vet him. When Paulus is confident that he would be a good prospect for adoption, he sends a broker to talk to the father of Timotheus.

The broker is the representative of Paulus and has the authority to do business on his behalf. He speaks to the father of Timotheus (let's give him the name Sergios) and proposes an adoption. He asks Sergios what the price would be. Now, why would Sergios have any interest in selling his son for adoption? There could be several reasons. Selling a son into adoption was different than selling a son into slavery. Children sold into slavery could be repurchased back out of slavery. Not so with adoption. So, certainly the price would be much higher. A family could have several sons and heirs and wouldn't need all their sons. They might have daughters for which money for dowries would have to be raised. And importantly, the family doing the adopting might offer wealth and opportunity beyond what he would have in his own family.

So, in our story, Sergios quotes an exorbitant price for Timotheus. The broker returns to Paulus with the news, and Paulus agrees, though the cost is very sacrificial—that is how badly Paulus wants a son. The broker returns with the money in hand to Sergios and a very interesting transaction takes place. Unlike slavery, where it is a simple exchange of money for the person, adoption requires a "three parts" transaction in the exchange. Not knowing exactly what this looks like, let's assume it is a "going once, going twice, done deal" type of exchange. At that moment, the word "*mancipatio*" takes effect. The word emancipation, or freedom, comes from this word. But in that context, it meant the *potesta* (authority) of Sergios was broken off of Timotheus.

We aren't done yet. One more step must be taken. The two fathers appear with the broker and Timotheus before the magistrate. There, they present all the facts and details about the execution of the transaction. When the magistrate is satisfied that the law has been met, he declares "*vindicatio*," from which we get the word vindication. But in this context, it means "*new birth.*" The adopted son has a new start in life. He has a new life, a new family, a new home, a new everything! His new life has begun. It also has these features:

- It is permanent—cannot be undone.

- In the eyes of the law, he is no longer who he was. He has a new identity.

- The new father, Paulus, assumes responsibilities for all of Timotheus's debts.

- He becomes an equal, joint heir with any other sons.

Metaphors are metaphors—they aren't perfect. But you can see why Paul used this metaphor to help these Gentile believers understand the transformation and exchange that happens when they are born again. With a little imagination, we can extrapolate some of this metaphor.

- The adopting father, Paulus, is Father God—who wanted more sons.

- Timotheus is us.

- The natural father, Sergios, represents the authority (*potestas*) of our former life—the world, Adam, Satan, etc.

- The broker is the Holy Spirit.

- The magistrate represents the demands of the law.

- Who is Jesus? The price that was paid!

We can also work with some other thoughts and ideas. We passed from death to life, from darkness to light, from bondage to freedom, from one authority to another. And yet sometimes we tend to think about the old days and the old neighborhood. We might even long for some of those things at times—like the children of Israel looking back at Egypt. That is exactly why our main exhortation and answer is the renewing of our mind.

And do not be conformed to this world but be transformed by the renewing of your mind, that you may prove what is that good and acceptable and perfect will of God. Romans 12:2

There is another very important part of this story as well. What did God have in mind in receiving us as sons through adoption? "For God so loved the world that He sent His only begotten son." Jesus is not the only begotten anymore! Now He is the first born among many brethren.

*For whom He foreknew, He also predestined to be conformed to the image of His Son, that He might be the **firstborn among many brethren**.* Romans 8:29

The only son became the first-born son. The first-person Jesus spoke to after His resurrection was Mary Magdalene. Among the many things that can be said about that passage, we will note one very significant thing—when Jesus called the disciples brethren:

*Jesus said to her, "Do not cling to Me, for I have not yet ascended to My Father; but go to **My brethren** and say to them, 'I am ascending to **My Father and your Father**, and to My God and your God.'"* John 20:17

This is the first time He has called them *brethren*. What has happened? The finished work on the cross, the tomb, and the resurrection—it changed everything for them and for us! He now had a different relationship with the disciples. He now could present His followers to the Father as sons, which made them His brethren. But we are just scratching the surface about sonship. Let's take a deeper look.

The word *brethren* is a great word! The Greek word is *adelphos*, meaning "unity of the womb. The most common name for a believer in the New Testament is saint. But when the scriptures talk about us in the Christian community, the most common name is brethren. We are all born, or have been begotten, out of the same womb! Jesus was begotten of the Father and so have we also been. The event that allowed for us to be able to be begotten in our new birth is the death and resurrection of Jesus.

> *Most assuredly, I say to you, unless a grain of wheat falls into the ground and dies, it remains alone; but if it dies, it produces much grain.* John 12:24

Jesus is many things to us. He is redeemer, savior, rescuer, Lord, healer, deliverer, and master. *But he is also our elder brother.* Jesus is not ashamed of this new relationship we have with Him, and he has a purpose and goal in mind. This profound passage in Hebrews makes many points.

> *For it was fitting for Him, for whom are all things and by whom are all things, in* bringing many sons to glory, *to make the captain of their salvation perfect through sufferings. For **both He who sanctifies and those who are being sanctified are all of one, for which reason He is not ashamed to call them brethren**, saying: "I will **declare Your name to My brethren**; In the midst of the assembly I will sing praise to You." And again: "I will put My trust in Him." And again*: "**Here am I and the children whom God has given Me**." *Inasmuch then as the children have partaken of flesh and blood, **He Himself likewise shared in the same**, that through death He might destroy him who had the power of death, that is, the devil,* Hebrews 2:10–14

1. Jesus is going to bring us to glory—finish what He started.*Being confident of this very thing, that He who has begun a good work in you will complete it until the day of Jesus Christ;* Philippians 1:6

    Therefore we also, since we are surrounded by so great a cloud of witnesses, let us lay aside every weight, and the sin which so easily ensnares us, and let us run with endurance the race that is set before us, looking unto Jesus, the author and finisher of our faith, who for the joy that was set before Him endured the cross, despising the shame, and has sat down at the right hand of the throne of God. Hebrews 12:1–2

2. He is the captain of our salvation, the forerunner. As our captain, He was made perfect (complete) through His own suffering. He had to go through what He went through to accomplish the totality of what He did. Nothing was left undone!

3. We are all of one—the Father!

4. He's not ashamed of us.

5. He declares the Father to us.

6. The Father gave us to Jesus—Jesus gives us to the Father! A lot of incredible giving is going on!

    The eyes of your understanding being enlightened; that you may know what is the hope of His calling, what are the riches of the glory of His inheritance in the saints...Ephesians 1:18

7. He shared in our humanity so that He could taste and destroy death!

Yes, we are sons. But we are also becoming sons. Sonship is both already and becoming. My Dad's name was Afton, though he went by Skeeter. He was a great man with many tremendous qualities, and he had a very good name and reputation. So naturally I really looked up to him and wanted to be like him. I was born his son on September 5, 1953. But the more I got to know him, the more his son I became. He passed away in 1995, but I am still his son and as I continue to mature, I look more and more like him. At the end of the day, he is not my ultimate model for sonship to grow by. I want to be more and more like my elder brother, Jesus, who is the perfect representation of the Father!

Chapter 7
THE NEW COVENANT

...not according to the covenant that I made with their fathers in the day that I took them by the hand to lead them out of the land of Egypt, My covenant which they broke, though I was a husband to them, says the Lord. But this is the covenant that I will make with the house of Israel after those days, says the Lord: I will put My law in their minds, and write it on their hearts; and I will be their God, and they shall be My people. No more shall every man teach his neighbor, and every man his brother, saying, 'Know the Lord,' for they all shall know Me, from the least of them to the greatest of them, says the Lord. For I will forgive their iniquity, and their sin I will remember no more.
JEREMIAH 31:32–34

When Rosanne and I stood at the altar and said our marriage vows on July 1, 1978, we were making covenant with each other. In our forty-five years of marriage, we have been learning about what happened that day, as God performed the miracle of us becoming one. That day a new "us" was created. There is still Bo and Rosanne, but the new *us* is a new creation that has its own personality, vision, dreams, and character. Believing in the miracle of becoming one and processing all experiences of our marriage through that truth has made our marriage an adventure, not an obstacle. It has been such a good ride and we both look forward to the next forty-five years!

Many Christians have little or no understanding that we are in covenant with God through Jesus Christ. We are in covenant because we are in Him, and He keeps the covenant for us, even when we are unfaithful. But finding out we are in covenant with God and coming to understand the wonderful aspects of the covenant is like finding out there is unlimited oil and gas riches below the land you just purchased. It just keeps getting better! Let's look at a few of the incredible facts of this truth of being in the New Covenant:

1. The NEW covenant has replaced the OLD covenant.

The book of Hebrews, written to Jewish believers, makes it very clear that the old covenant of justification by works is obsolete and fading away, and it has been replaced by the New Covenant prophesied in Jeremiah 31. The Old Covenant has been replaced by a better one. The blood of bulls and goats could never remove our sins but could only cover them for a limited time period. We have a new High Priest, Jesus, who not only enters the holiest place for us but offers the sacrifice of His own blood which satisfies the penalty for sin forever. The following passage sums up the power and efficacy of the New Covenant:

> And every priest stands ministering daily and offering repeatedly the same sacrifices, which can never take away sins. But this Man, after He had offered one sacrifice for sins forever, sat down at the right hand of God, from that time waiting till His enemies are made His footstool. For by one offering He has perfected forever those who are being sanctified. But the Holy Spirit also witnesses to us; for after He had said before, "This is the covenant that I will make with them after those days, says the Lord: I will put My laws into their hearts, and in their minds I will write them," then He adds, "Their sins

and their lawless deeds I will remember no more." Now where there is remission of these, there is no longer an offering for sin. Therefore, brethren, having boldness to enter the Holiest by the blood of Jesus, by a new and living way which He consecrated for us, through the veil, that is, His flesh, and having a High Priest over the house of God, let us draw near with a true heart in full assurance of faith, having our hearts sprinkled from an evil conscience and our bodies washed with pure water. Let us hold fast the confession of our hope without wavering, for He who promised is faithful. Hebrews 10:11-23

Man's first efforts to get right with God, or the first religion, was to clothe himself with coverings made from fig leaves. God replaced the fig leaves with animal skins for covering their nakedness, which required the shedding of blood. The Mosaic Covenant required a system of animal sacrifices which provided temporary and partial atonement that could never take away sins. But finally, Jesus's perfect sacrifice has for all time redeemed those who put their faith in His finished work.

2. **We are in covenant, not in a contract.**

Contracts are made between two parties and can be broken by either party. In the New covenant, we are in covenant through a representative, Christ. We are represented by our representative. The genius of God was the incarnation of Christ. God provided a sinless representation that could and would pay the price for our sins in a onetime act of sacrifice. But we would be included in His sacrifice so we could be raised up and included in His life.

Let this mind be in you which was also in Christ Jesus, who, being in the form of God, did not consider it robbery to be equal with God, but made Himself of no reputation, taking the form of a bondservant, and coming in the likeness of men. And being found in appearance as a man, He humbled Himself and became obedient to the point of death, even the death of the cross. Therefore God also has highly exalted Him and given Him the name which is above every name, that at the name of Jesus every knee should bow, of those in heaven, and of those on earth, and of those under the earth, and that every tongue should confess that Jesus Christ is Lord, to the glory of God the Father. Philippians 2:5–11

3.   This covenant is a blood covenant.

There are other types of covenants in biblical history, but the strongest is the blood covenant. It is made by the oath of God. God chose to make covenant with Himself. There was not some emptiness in Him that required Him to fill it—He is complete. When He says, "I will never leave you or forsake you," He is stating the immutable truth of His being. We can trust what He says. It is a unilateral covenant that God makes with Himself. It was initiated and fulfilled by God. We are included in the covenant that God made with Himself by His own blood. The blood of Christ satisfies the demands of a holy God and will for all eternity. Because I am in Christ, my sins are already atoned for, even the ones I haven't yet committed. This is an oath God has made with Himself—it is why He says, "Their sins I will remember no more." The word for forgiveness is *aphiemi,* which means to send away, to dismiss, to forsake, to leave—remembered no more.

And every priest stands ministering daily and offering repeatedly the same sacrifices, which can never take away sins. But this Man, after He had offered one sacrifice for sins forever, sat down at the right hand of God, from that time waiting till His enemies are made His footstool. For by one offering He has perfected forever those who are being sanctified. Hebrews 10:11–14

Watchman Nee speaks of the blood being directed first toward God, second toward us, and third toward Satan. The blood is primarily for God. When we sin, God does not overlook what we have done wrong, but He is satisfied by the blood. Nee says, *"If I want to understand the value of the blood I must accept God's valuation of it."* [4] Our valuation of it must be nothing more or less than God's. So, the blood likewise applies to my conscience in the same way. My conscience is that inner voice that judges me when I do wrong. It finds me guilty and has no power to cleanse me. That is why the blood applied to my conscience gives me an updated valuation of God's value for the blood. His blood has cleansed me. Who am I to say that it must be cleansed some other way? Satan knows this truth about the blood, yet he accuses us to ourselves because he knows the power of shame to cripple us. Having been forgiven, we can declare our righteousness to Satan to shut him up.

4. This covenant is based on chesed, the lovingkindness of God.

Chesed is the Hebrew word for grace, but it is most often translated as lovingkindness or mercy. Rosanne and I entered into a marriage covenant so that we could create lovingkindness for each other and so that lovingkindness would grow as our marriage matured. God created the New Covenant to reveal His lovingkindness. It is not something He has—it is who He is! This is why we can be assured and confident of our relationship with Him. It is never based on our performance, but on what Jesus accomplished for us. The only thing required of us is having faith to believe.

> *But Christ came as High Priest of the good things to come, with the greater and more perfect tabernacle not made with hands, that is, not of this creation. Not with the blood of goats and calves, but with His own blood He entered the Most Holy Place once for all,*

4   Nee, Watchman. (1977) *The Normal Christian Life*, Tyndale House

having obtained eternal redemption. For if the blood of bulls and goats and the ashes of a heifer, sprinkling the unclean, sanctifies for the purifying of the flesh, how much more shall the blood of Christ, who through the eternal Spirit offered Himself without spot to God, cleanse your conscience from dead works to serve the living God? And for this reason He is the Mediator of the new covenant, by means of death, for the redemption of the transgressions under the first covenant, that those who are called may receive the promise of the eternal inheritance. Hebrews 9:11–15

5. **Christ is our representative in the making and keeping of the covenant.**

He is our mediator. He is the last Adam and the second man. When something is last, there is no more. There will not be another Adam that supersedes Christ. He has put an end to the race of Adam and He is the beginning of a new humanity as the second man. He is the apostle of God to humankind, and He is our High Priest, representing us to God. He is the perfect and complete keeper of the covenant. He will never fail us or forsake us or abandon us. He sympathizes with us in our weakness, and He is committed to bringing all of us as sons to glory.

For such a High Priest was fitting for us, who is holy, harmless, undefiled, separate from sinners, and has become higher than the heavens; who does not need daily, as those high priests, to offer up sacrifices, first for His own sins and then for the people's, for this He did once for all when He offered up Himself. For the law appoints as high priests men who have weakness, but the word of the oath, which came after the law, appoints the Son who has been perfected forever. Now this is the main point of the things we are saying: We have such a High Priest, who is seated at the right hand of the throne of the Majesty in the heavens, a Minister of the sanctuary and of the true tabernacle which the Lord erected, and not man. Hebrews 7:26–8:2

6. The New Covenant operates according to law.

Daily life in the New Covenant is based on choices we make. We either live by the law of the Spirit of life in Christ or by the law of the flesh, or of sin and death.

> *There is therefore now no condemnation to those who are in Christ Jesus, For the law of the Spirit of life in Christ Jesus has made me free from the law of sin and death. Romans 8:1,2*

> *For those who live according to the flesh set their minds on the things of the flesh, but those who live according to the Spirit, the things of the Spirit. For to be carnally minded is death, but to be spiritually minded is life and peace. Romans 8:5–6*

As we have discussed many times in this book, life in the Spirit begins with *knowing*, but it doesn't end there. It leads to *reckoning* (believing) and then *presenting ourselves* to God (obeying) and then walking the "walk" of our new life. Life in the New Covenant is life in Christ and Christ's life in us. We have been joined to Him and derive our life from Him.

When we choose the flesh and sin, we aren't taken out of the covenant because we have been sealed in Christ. But those actions are a betrayal of who we are and there are always consequences for our sin. The consequence is not rejection or eternal judgment from God, but the natural result of reaping what we have sown. The fallen world we live in is always ready to give us our due reaping!

7. We cannot add anything to this covenant.

We can't make it better, richer, or more effective. This has been accomplished by Christ on our behalf. Our part is to completely surrender and accept and believe by faith that it is complete. To think that we need to add something to make our salvation more complete or secure is to say that Jesus' atonement is inadequate. This is not a performance agreement between us and God. Having said that, when we completely surrender to His finished work, our life is exchanged for His and we LIVE DIFFERENTLY! It is a progressive experience.

For by grace you have been saved through faith, and that not of yourselves; it is the gift of God, not of works, lest anyone should boast. For we are His workmanship, created in Christ Jesus for good works, which God prepared beforehand that we should walk in them. Ephesians 2:8-10

The idea of workmanship is not automatic but takes place over time. We are given His righteousness, but we also grow into His righteousness. It is always His righteousness, but we come to look more and more like Him over time. So, the works we do are a result of and not a cause to make it happen.

8. **We have been sealed in Christ by the Holy Spirit of promise, not only for our present reality but for all that is to come! There is an eternal future to this covenant!**

In Him you also trusted, after you heard the word of truth, the gospel of your salvation; in whom also, having believed, you were sealed with the Holy Spirit of promise, who is the guarantee of our inheritance until the redemption of the purchased possession, to the praise of His glory. Ephesians 1:13–14

When God seals us, it means we are held in covenant by Him, not by ourselves. Who can break God's seal? We certainly don't have the power or authority to undo what we couldn't do in the first place!

We have only scratched the surface in our understanding of the New Covenant. But covenantal language and truth is a weapon we can use against the accusations and attacks of the enemy. It is truth we can quote to the enemy to shut him up. It is truth that sets us free—not only from the penalty of sin but from the power of sin. When we refresh our spirit and soul in this truth, we are strengthened and girded to run the race set before us. We are not just recipients of the benefits of this covenant, we have been transformed and made to be overcomers for nothing can stand against the truth and power of God!

This ends part one of our pursuit to know the truth about who we are in Christ and what we have in Him. Jesus said, *"And you shall know the truth, and the truth shall make you free"* [5] Three takeaways from that scripture are: 1) We CAN know the truth. 2) If there is truth, then we can also know error—we don't want that! 3) Knowing truth gives us freedom while error gives us bondage.

We want to know the truth! A primary purpose of this book is to expose errors and reveal the truth. It must begin with getting our own personal revelation of who we are in Christ as a result of what He has done in His finished work, changing forever who we are and what we have.

What you have read thus far of my story and how God began to reveal truth to me in my faith journey might help you. But my revelation can't take the place of you receiving your own. And as my journey continued, I had to confront some old and long-held beliefs that were being challenged. I had some tough questions I needed answers to.

---

5   John 8:32

Part 2

UNTYING THE KNOTS

I have always encouraged people to take their biblical literacy seriously, especially people in ministry leadership. I even suggest that people work out their own personal theology. That can be a daunting task with so many variations on theology. But the hunt is worth it. By pursuing an understanding of various theological themes and subjects, a person is more exposed to what is out there than if they don't.

In the telling of my story, I had been a believer for about thirty-five years when the life group began our study of Grace and the New Man. So, I had a personal theology pretty much worked out. I didn't have everything figured out for sure, but what I did have figured out I was sure about. Wow was I ever wrong! Some of my theology was being challenged. I've learned to be open when the Holy Spirit presses us about beliefs we hold. Remember, the Teacher lives inside of us. But as some of my theology system was being challenged and new understanding was taking place, I had to do something with my old questions.

This section in the book is included to not only share more about my learning and growing process, but perhaps to help you with some of your questions. In the chapters of this section are proposed answers to common questions. You may find some of these easy and some difficult, but all have value. I propose answers to these questions with humility and sincerity. I make no apology for my effort, but I do make a disclaimer. My disclaimer is this—I am not a theologian. The Church is a big tent with lots of views held by good people of faith. I may be wrong about some things in some of my answers, but I give them to you with honesty and challenge you to consider them.

Chapter 8
WHAT HAS SIN DONE TO US?

...for all have sinned and fall short of the glory of God.
ROMANS 3:23

One of my favorite movies as a boy was "The Great Escape." I still love to watch it today. It was masterfully produced, telling a true story about the escape of about 120 allied prisoners from a German POW camp. One of the characters in the story was Roger. He loved birds and especially drawing them. Having great artistic talent, he was given the job of forging papers for the escapees. Unfortunately, Roger and most of the escapees were recaptured and many lost their lives, but his exacting talent did help some make it to freedom.

Roger forged identities to help his friends, but identity forgery is not usually a good thing. Identity theft is one of the most talked about challenges we all face. There are some good scammers out in the cyber world who are very smart and capable of stealing identities or getting into secure places such as bank accounts. I hear ads for "home title theft" safeguard programs all the time. But the master identity theft villain has always been Satan. He is a thief and robber, and he has been developing his craft at our expense for thousands of years. He couldn't abort the work of Christ, so he is trying to rob us of living in its benefits by deceiving us about who we are.

If we don't know who we are, how can we live the life God intends for us? If we think we are someone or something different than what the Bible says about us, we are inclined to live up to what we believe. Sometimes I would tell my kids, "Williams don't do that!" or, "This is what we do because this is who we are!"

Every person either chooses to be in Adam or in Christ. Once a person decides to give their life to Christ, their identity is changed forever. Once our identity is changed, we choose to believe it, or not. What we believe about who we are is consequential. I made my choice to be in Christ fifty-one years ago, but for 35 years I lived in identity confusion! As I have said, I struggled to reign in life much of the time as I was focused on managing my failure. In this chapter on sin, it will help us to rightly understand the effect of sin so we can understand what Christ had to accomplish in His finished work.

In the New Testament, *sinner* is found 86 times, almost all of which occur in the gospels. Only a few times is *sinner* found in the epistles. The reason being that in the epistles, the finished work of Christ has occurred, and for those who choose life in Him, they are now saints—remember? Many Christians find themselves "sin conscious," very focused on overcoming sin. Their thoughts and energy are spent on resisting and saying no.

The better focus is to be life conscious—Christ living His life in us and through us. If our thinking and energy focus is toward God and the leading of the Holy Spirit, there is little to no room for thoughts of sin to affect us.

Even so, sin is still important to rightly understand so it can be effectively dealt with. Watchman Nee draws a distinction between *sin* singular and *sins* plural. He states that sin is a condition of the nature of man that must be dealt with, while sins are my individual acts that must be atoned for. Romans 1-5:11 deals primarily with my *sins* and forgiveness, accomplished by the blood of Christ. Romans 5:12-8:39 deals primarily with *sin and our sin nature*, accomplished by the cross. Jesus's blood provided forgiveness for my acts of sin and makes me clean. But the cross deals with who I am in Adam and makes me a new person. I needed to be forgiven and cleansed from what I have done, but I also needed to be delivered from who I was. Jesus bore our sins on the cross, now His cross must bear me, the sinner. Nee says that Jesus's death and shed blood provided the dual remedy. Let's take a further look at sin.

THE ORIGIN OF SIN

Much has been written or said about the fall of Adam and Eve. This short section intends to hit a few highlights of their fateful decision. They were created in the image of God, from dust. God breathed into Adam the breath of life, which originates from God Himself. They were in perfect fellowship with God and all provision for life was prepared and given to them. They had dominion over creation and were charged with the stewardship of all God had made. They were given two commandments. The first command was to be fruitful and multiply and govern. The second command prohibited eating of the fruit of just one of the trees in the garden. They could eat of any tree *except for the tree of the knowledge of good and evil.*

They had everything they needed, and they had it good! They also had free will, freedom to choose. Because they had been given responsibility to multiply and steward creation, they had to choose to do that. Because they had been given a line not to cross in eating fruit from the forbidden tree, they had to choose to not cross that line. And because they were in relationship with God who was over them, they were subject to these commands. They were dependent on God who was greater than them. As long as they chose correctly, their innocence was intact and protected. Then, temptation entered the garden:

> *Now the serpent was more cunning than any beast of the field which the Lord God had made. And he said to the woman, "Has God*

indeed said, 'You shall not eat of every tree of the garden'?" And the woman said to the serpent, "We may eat the fruit of the trees of the garden; but of the fruit of the tree which is in the midst of the garden, God has said, 'You shall not eat it, nor shall you touch it, lest you die.' " Then the serpent said to the woman, "You will not surely die. For God knows that in the day you eat of it your eyes will be opened, and you will be like God, knowing good and evil." So when the woman saw that the tree was good for food, that it was pleasant to the eyes, and a tree desirable to make one wise, she took of its fruit and ate. She also gave to her husband with her, and he ate. Genesis 3:1–6

Temptation originates from Satan, the adversary, who has set himself against God and His kingdom, wanting to rule his own kingdom. Temptation is his domain—then and now. When we are tempted today, it is the same essence of this temptation in the garden. It begins with a crafty lie. It is crafty in the sense that part of it is true, which strengthens the deception.

Later John would write in his first epistle, *Do not love the world or the things in the world. If anyone loves the world, the love of the Father is not in him. For all that is in the world*—**the lust of the flesh, the lust of the eyes, and the pride of life**—*is not of the Father but is of the world*—1 John 2:15,16. John was probably thinking of the story in Genesis when he wrote those lines. The lust of the flesh—good for food; lust of the eyes—pleasant to behold; and the pride of life—desirable to make one wise, like God.

She also gave to her husband with her, and he ate. The immediate result was the loss of their innocence and the beginning of guilt and shame. Desperate to cover their nakedness, they made coverings of fig leaves sewn together. What a feeble and inadequate answer to their problem! I joke that their fig leaf underwear wouldn't stand a chance in our west Texas winds!

The covering of fig leaves was man's first religion—self effort to be right with God. Of course, God came along and covered them with skins from animals which required the shedding of blood. Here, we see two things, grace in action to cover man's sin, and a type of Christ's sacrifice that will bring redemption and salvation. So much more could be said about the event in Genesis 3 but let us move on to look more intently at the DNA of when sin entered the world.

THE NATURE OF SIN

The organic nature of sin is "I will." Adam and Eve were created to be in relationship with God in a dependent, subservient condition. They had everything they needed or could want, except for eternal life. It is a theological debate as to when or how they would have entered eternal life. Was it when they would eat from the Tree of Life? They were banished from the garden so that they couldn't eat from it. God set an eternal plan in motion that would remedy the problem of sin.

The "I will" nature is a condition of being independent. There are types of independence. There is the independence seen in a child learning to tie his shoes and he frustratingly says, "I can do this—let me do it!" There is the independent attitude of the man who goes into business for himself, so he doesn't have to answer to anyone but himself. There is the unfulfilled mother who seeks to enter the workplace to achieve something society places more value on than being hidden at home. These forms of independence are not necessarily wrong.

But in relation to God, independence develops into increasingly more toxic conditions. The person who prefers a hedonistic lifestyle over Christian living is a classic picture. Less obvious are those who desire to control and manage the details of living, including achievement and accomplishment. Many people are motivated by a search for meaning, especially being recognized and rewarded by society. We live in an achievement/reward culture that is the driver of what most successful people strive for. Few people, Christian or non-Christian, make place for some type of sabbath observance where nothing is measured.

Choices. We make them every day. Some choices are thought out, but many are spontaneous. Some choices we make to satisfy some desire or appetite of the flesh. Some we make to invest in something good for us or others. Some we make based on truth as given to us from God's word, but some we make based on the world's truth, which are lies of the enemy, intended to deceive us.

As we have learned, when we were born again, we ended the reign of Adam's existence for us. Our identity in him was dealt a death blow and he is buried in the tomb. He is no more. But God's work on the cross didn't end the effect of sin in our lives. We still contend with it, though from a different position and with the hope of a very different outcome.

THE CONSEQUENCES OF SIN

Sin represents the difference between all God is and all we are on our own without God. Sometimes people are evil sinners—there is nothing good in them. They are mean, self-centered, hateful, spiteful, dishonest, and perhaps even violent.

Sometimes people are "good" sinners, people who are pleasant, kind, generous, and honest. Perhaps they were taught good values at home or have learned along the way the biblical principle of sowing and reaping.— kindness begets kindness, etc.

Most people care about their reputation—what others think of them. They choose the option to live a life with some meaning and value. They want to have a purpose or a path in life that amounts to something. They want to leave this world having made a mark and leave it in a better condition due to their efforts. You know people like this. Perhaps this is what used to drive you. They busy themselves in organizations and charities and efforts that do-good things for someone or something. And perhaps they get enough accolades to affirm their efforts. But they are independent of God and do good things out of their soul. The outworking of independence from God ranges from good people doing their own thing to evil people exploiting others for pleasure or profit. The nature of sin is "I will."

When I was being witnessed to by my college friends, I was told verbally and through tracts that my sin separated me from God and I was in a state of spiritual death. Though I thought I was a "good" person, I realized all my goodness was not good enough. The simple definition for the most common Greek word for sin, *Hamartia*, means missing the mark. But N.T. Wright says, "Sin (hamartia) is bigger than simply breaking the rules. It is a failure to be genuinely human by bearing the image of God in the earth."[6] When we fail to bear His image we miss the mark, whether we miss it by a little or a lot.

If the two categories of sinner, the good person sinner and the evil person sinner represent opposite ends of a range, most people will fall somewhere in between on the continuum. But wherever you are on this scale, **you need a redeemer!** Everyone does. Remember Romans 3:23— *for all have sinned and fall short of the glory of God,*.

IMBEDDED SIN

One of the most insidious issues of sin is sin that originates from the inside that is hidden to us because of a lack of understanding of the nature and power of sin. This can best be understood in looking at some of the Greek words for love. The words for family love (*storge*) and friendship love (*phileo*) are not the big issue, but two other words are—*agape* (unconditional love) and *eros* (sexual love). *Agape* is the Septuagint's translation of the Hebrew word *ahav*, which is God's love toward us and is an unconditional love based on choice and not feeling. *Agape* is love that is turned outward and away from us. It seeks the benefit of the recipient, even at a

6   Wright, N.T. (2005). *Paul, A Fresh Perspective*, Fortress

cost to us. God loves us with *agape* love and because we have been made new and given a new heart, we have the capacity to love ourselves and others with *agape* love.

But *eros*, as the word for sexual love, had its origins in Greek mythology and pagan erotic religions. In its context as sexual love, the word has a strong component of selfishness imbedded in its meaning. The essence of the meaning of *eros* is the desire to possess or control something or someone. *Eros*, due to its inherent selfish nature, is the basic commonality of all sin. *Eros* can manifest itself as a perspective of seeing oneself as the center of the universe, either overtly or subtly. *Eros* is a form of love whose only goal is to get its own needs met.

Bob Mumford, in his excellent book, *Agape Road*, contrasts *agape* and *eros* with three types of arrows. A straight arrow, pointing away from us, is the *agape* arrow—focused on the needs of others. An arrow curved and pointing back to us like a hook is *eros*—representing that *eros* always seeks its own benefit, always turning everything to itself. But the third arrow is a mixed arrow, with both a forward direction and a returning direction, reflecting that we have some of both in our lives. Mumford describes something he calls the *eros* virus. Our tendency toward selfishness and sin can mutate into different forms as we live life. About the time we feel like we've conquered selfishness, it simply mutates and reappears in another form and place. How true this is!

Selfishness is a focus on us, and it is more insidious than we might think at first glance. L.E. Maxwell describes the influence of self in this way—"The victorious believer will become aware of many forms of self which must yet be dealt with. We shall discover:

- In our service for Christ; self-confidence and self-esteem,
- In the slightest suffering; self-saving and self-pity,
- In the least misunderstanding; self-defense and self-vindication,
- In our station in life; self-seeking and self-centeredness,

- In the daily routine; self-pleasing and self-choosing,
- In our relationships; self-assertiveness and self-respect,
- In our education; self-boasting and self-expression,
- In our desires; self-indulgence and self-satisfaction
- In our successes; self-admiration and self-congratulation,
- In our failures; self-excusing and self-justification,
- In our spiritual attainments; self-righteousness and self-complacency,
- In our public ministry; self-reflection and self-glory"[7]

Wow! What a list! This is why the renewing of the mind is so critical and never ending. Our mind is the headquarters of our will, making the many moment by moment decisions we live out. The more we think with the mind of Christ, the more we make right decisions. *The life of Christ in us is the mind of Christ in us—thinking as we should and can.* The renewing of our mind requires us to think right. We can do this! Thinking the thoughts of God comes from abiding in Him and His words abiding in us. More will be said in a later chapter, but you can think like Christ!

In the original sin, Adam and Eve became overdeveloped in their soul. They stepped from dependence on God to independence from God. Again, prepositions matter. They were no longer of God, but now they were of man. On that fateful day, a race of humanity began that would propagate the same independent nature. Seth was Adam's third son and scripture says that he was begotten in the image of Adam. *And Adam lived one hundred and thirty years, and begot a son in his own likeness, after his image, and named him Seth*—Genesis 5: 3. This was the beginning of the progeny from Adam, the race of humanity in the nature of Adam, with the independent spirit. Before Christ, we are image-bearers of Adam.

---

7 Maxwell, L.E. (2010). *Born Crucified*, Moody

THE SOLUTION FOR SIN

I reached the point in my faith decision where I knew I was facing two paths. One path was a self-path that would develop me as a good person wanting to live a good life but independent from God. The other path was God's path. He had been drawing me to Him by His love. I had come to believe that I could choose a life in Him that would be the right and best choice by far. I didn't want empty. I wanted fullness. So, I chose the other path, the path of life. Yes, I knew that my eternal destination was heaven, but I was honestly more focused on abundant life now, a life of purpose and destiny—His destiny. So, I chose Christ. Though I immediately was aware of a personal relationship with Christ, the outworking of my new identity was only beginning. Though I was "all new," the realization and understanding of newness has been increasing ever since.

Scripture gives us an incredible picture of the transformation from Adam to Christ in Romans chapter five, where our old life in Adam is directly compared to our new life in Christ. Here it follows:

*For when we were still without strength, in due time **Christ died for the ungodly.***

*For scarcely for a righteous man will one die; yet perhaps for a good man someone would even dare to die. But God demonstrates His own love toward us, in that **while we were still sinners, Christ died for us.** Much more then, having now been justified by His blood, we shall be saved from wrath through Him. For if when we were enemies we were reconciled to God through the death of His Son, **much more, having been reconciled, we shall be saved by His life.** And not only that, but we also rejoice in God through our Lord Jesus Christ, through whom we have now received the reconciliation. Therefore, just **as through one man sin entered the world,** and **death through sin,** and thus **death spread to all men, because all sinned**—(For until the law sin was in the world, but sin is not* *imputed when there is no law. Nevertheless* **death reigned from Adam to Moses**, *even over those who had not sinned according to the likeness of the transgression of Adam, who is a type of Him who was to come.* **But the free gift is not like the offense.** *For if by* **the one man's offense many died**, *much more* **the grace of God and the gift by the grace of the one Man, Jesus Christ, abounded to many.** *And the gift is not like that which came through the one who sinned. For* **the judgment which came from one offense resulted in condemnation,** *but* **the free gift which came from many offenses resulted in justification.** *For if* **by the one man's offense death reigned** *through the one, much* **more those who receive abundance of grace and of the gift of righteousness will reign in life through the One, Jesus Christ.)** *Therefore, as through* **one man's offense judgment came to all men, resulting in condemnation,** *even so* **through one Man's righteous act the free gift came to all men, resulting in justification of life. For as by one man's disobedience many were made sinners,** *so also by* **one Man's obedience many will be made righteous.** *Moreover the law entered that the offense might abound.* **But where sin abounded, grace abounded much more,** *so that as* **sin reigned in death,** *even so* **grace might reign through righteousness to eternal life through Jesus Christ our Lord.** Romans 5:6–21

Wow! What a contrast. It is even more dramatic if we make two lists—one under Adam, which represents who we used to be and what we possessed, contrasted to the list of who we are now and what we possess in Christ. The Adam list is NO more while the Christ list is our new truth!

Adam (Past)	Christ (present and future)
Helpless	Loved
Ungodly	Justified
Sinners	Saved
Wrath	Reconciled
Enemies of God	Free gift
Sin and death	Reigning in life
Spreading death	Grace of God
All sinned	Abound to many
Transgression	Abundance of grace
Condemnation	Justification of life
Death reigned	Grace would reign
Disobedience of the one	Obedience of the one
Made sinners	Made righteous

This isn't a changed life. It certainly isn't a "better" life. It is an EXCHANGED life. It is different in every respect!

Chapter 9
WHY DO I STILL STRUGGLE?

But now, it is no longer I who do it, but sin that dwells in
me. For I know that in me (that is, in my flesh) nothing good
dwells; for to will is present with me, but how to perform
what is good I do not find. For the good that I will to do, I
do not do; but the evil I will not to do, that I practice.
ROMANS 7:17-19

I was serious about my relationship with Christ from day one. That doesn't mean I didn't have my very self -centered days, but my over-all disposition toward my life in Christ, my witness, how I saw myself internally and how others saw me externally was very serious to me. I was fully bought in. The scriptures about taking up my cross daily meant something to me. But I still struggled in certain areas of temptation. And when I say I struggled, I wasn't just tempted, I sinned.

There were areas of my life that changed dramatically right away for sure, and I was excited about those changes. Looking back, it is clear to me that those changes were the low hanging fruit of repentance. I lost my appetite for partying, for example. I had a heightened sense of honesty and right and wrong and it was relatively easy to make those choices. But there were other sinful areas that had deeper roots—sexual temptation, fears, anxieties about certain things, vain thinking, pride, etc. It bothered me considerably when I failed in those areas. For the first thirty years of my life of faith, the question, "Why do I still struggle?" exasperated me to the point that I accepted a level of defeat as inevitable—something I would never be able to fully overcome.

Subconsciously, I came to believe that I would always fail on some level. So, if I was going to fail, I would make sure that my failure was minimized and controlled. Without realizing what I was doing, I *was managing my sin failure*. In other words, I managed the level I would allow myself to fail—I couldn't let it get too bad.

I think a lot of Christians do this without realizing what they are doing. What did that look like for me? I wasn't going to allow myself to become addicted to pornography, but I would allow myself to flirt with soft porn up to a certain point. I would never commit adultery, but I would entertain impure thoughts. I pre-empted fear by building up financial reserves or over controlling expenditures. Though I was serious about being a Christian, I had a lot of knots that needed to be untied. I had become a *sin manager,* and I was pretty good at it. The fundamental problem with sin management is allowing sin to keep a foothold in your life and not taking dominion over it. When sin has dominion over you it is clearly bondage. But the truth is that we have been set free of sin's dominion over us.

> *For sin shall not have dominion over you, for you are not under law but under grace.* Romans 6:14

In this same chapter where Paul explains our being united with Christ and our victory over sin, he twice addresses the question of whether we can keep sinning since grace abounds. So obviously there was an issue in his day of Christians being overcome by sin and of the false notion that grace empowers permissiveness. This will be addressed more in a later chapter, but here we need to resolve the question, *"why do I still struggle?"*

Remember, who we were as sinners was dealt with on the cross. But sin was not eradicated. Lest we think there is no struggle, or to say it another way, the battle is over, think again. There are many scriptures that *exhort us to put on our armor, resist the enemy, gird ourselves and to stand fast,* to name a few. There must be answers to the problem. Truthfully, we cannot be passive about living our life in Christ, but active, diligent, wise, and persistent. We are still in contention with both external and internal influences.

The first list of influences we contend with is **external** to us:

- Satan, the ruler of this world and demonic activity. He is our tempter.

- We live in a fallen world with its own ruler (Satan) and its own truth. He is a **deceiver**.

- **Sin** abounds in this fallen world. Temptation and the effect of sin surrounds us on every side.

Our enemy is highly committed to disrupting God's plan for our lives through deception and temptation. Satan failed to abort the seed of the promised Messiah, so he seeks to rob us of our inheritance. So, Satan and his demons try to influence us through temptation and deception. But the ruler of this world system does not have the power or authority to make us do anything. He is a liar, and the truth is not in him. He has been defeated as it relates to us. He is a bully that cowers in fear when we declare the truth of who we are in Christ.

Our bigger issue is internal to us—*our flesh and self.* We still have a flesh, or self, **not to be confused** with our old nature in Adam. They are NOT one and the same. *Our old self, our old nature in Adam, was crucified with Christ and left in the tomb when we were raised up in new life.* This is a very clear teaching in scripture as we have seen. It permeates Paul's letters. The consistency of this truth is written all through the New Testament. So, what is the flesh and self if it is not our old nature?

These two internal influences are the result of immaturity due to an unrenewed mind. Each of us might be mature in some areas but immature in others. As we continue to look at this, be thinking about areas of struggle you still have.

Now let's look at flesh and self and see what scripture says about it.

MY FLESH

If my old man has been crucified, buried, and is still in the grave, why are there scriptures that refer to my flesh in the present tense? For example, *And I, brethren, could not speak to you as to spiritual men, but as to **men of flesh**, as to infants in Christ. I gave you milk to drink, not solid food; for you were not yet able to receive it. Indeed, even now you are not yet able, for you are **still fleshly**. For since there is jealousy and strife among you, are you not fleshly, and are you not walking like mere men?* 1 Corinthians 3:1-3 (NASB)

The above scripture speaks both to issues of immaturity and to fleshly behavior. Unfortunately, there are Bible translations that sometimes translate flesh *(sarx)* as sin nature, instead of flesh. That isn't translation, that is interpretation. The word *sarx* is flesh– not *sin nature*. Sometimes it is translated as *carnal*, which is a good translation.

Paul in chapter 1, verse 2 of 1 Corinthians identifies these fleshly believers of Corinthians as *"saints."* He is careful to accurately state their **identity** before he writes the rest of his letter, which is filled with rebuke and correction and instruction concerning their **behavior**. Yes, even us saints sometimes live carnally, fleshly lives, which Paul carefully points out, is wrong! It isn't natural for us anymore! So, how are we to understand that we have been freed from the nature and dominion of Adam, and raised up a new creation in Christ—but we still must contend with our flesh?

We all have a *flesh*, and it ranges from a neutral, physical body to the seat of wrong passions and desires. Paul used it both ways. He referred to flesh as our mortal body in 2 Corinthians 4:11, and to the marital union of one flesh in Ephesians 5:31. But he also often spoke of flesh as the seat of sinful passions and desires, as in, *For those who* **live according to the flesh set their minds on the things of the flesh**, *but those who live according to the Spirit, the things of the Spirit. For to be carnally minded is death, but to be spiritually minded is life and peace. Because the carnal mind is enmity against God; for it is not subject to the law of God, nor indeed can be. So then,* **those who are in the flesh** *cannot please God.* Romans 8:5-8

His characterization of flesh as the cause of sinful passions is rooted in Greek philosophy that began with Epicurus a few hundred years prior to Paul. Paul was using language to help explain the human experience in answering the question, "*Why do I still struggle?*" so, he borrows from Greek philosophy to do so.

What is the answer to our flesh? In Galatians, Paul says that we who belong to Christ have crucified the flesh with its passions and desires. The answer to fleshly sinful desires is death. And we are the ones who are doing the crucifying! To better understand, let's look at four different references to crucifixion in Galatians:

1. Jesus was crucified (3:1),

2. I was crucified in Jesus when I was born again (2:20),

3. I am crucified to the world and the world to me (I am dead to the world and the world is dead to me, 6:14).

These three crucifixions apply *to* me; but, they are not done *by* me, they are done *for* me. I could not crucify myself—no one can. Jesus laid down His life, but he was crucified by Roman soldiers. However, the fourth reference to crucifixion is different:

4. I crucify MY flesh. It is an act of my will to crucify my own flesh—to take authority over it, rendering it without the power to entice me.

But the fruit of the Spirit is love, joy, peace, longsuffering, kindness, goodness, faithfulness, gentleness, self-control. Against such there is no law. **And those who are Christ's have crucified the flesh with its passions and desires.** *If we live in the Spirit, let us also walk in the Spirit. Galatians 5:22–25*

The unique feature of the flesh being crucified is that WE have done the crucifying. We didn't crucify our old nature. But with our flesh, we do. The answer to dealing with our flesh is reckoning the old man dead and reckoning the new man alive in the Spirit. Let me illustrate. I'm sitting at home alone watching a television program when an unexpected sex scene comes on the screen. Do I watch it? After all, it probably isn't going to show too much, I could reason. It will be over in a minute or two. Or do I use the remote control to change the channel or fast forward past the scene? My flesh wants to watch it. But if I do, those images will stick with me.

When I exercise my will in agreement with my identity, I make the right decision not to watch the scene, or perhaps even the program. I can even say these words out loud, *"I am not going to watch this. I don't do that anymore because that is not who I am. I am a new man in Christ and I have dominion over that temptation—it DOES NOT have dominion over me."*

This may seem like a silly example or even gimmicky, but I can guarantee you that it works because it aligns our will with the truth of our identity:

Therefore we also, since we are surrounded by so great a cloud of witnesses, **let us lay aside every weight, and the sin which so easily ensnares us,** *and let us run with endurance the race that is set before us, Hebrews 12:1*

What is the sin that so easily trips you up? Is it sexual temptation, greed, envy, jealousy, or anger? Is it worry and fear? Is it coveting? Whatever it is, there is a simple answer to it. You have dominion over it, not the other way around. We must also remember that it is by the *power of the Holy Spirit* that we exercise our will. Self-control is a fruit of the Spirit! Yes, you can crucify the flesh and walk in victory!

Because of what Jesus had done in us and for us, we can have freedom not only from the penalty of sin but the power of sin. This truth is all through the New Testament letters. You can know the truth that sets you free! Now, let's look at the second of these three things we contend with, self.

SELF

Self, like flesh, is found in scripture contexts that varies between positive, neutral, and negative. For example, we are told to *love our neighbor as we love ourselves.* What does it mean to love ourselves? We should love our new self in Christ. Our redeemed self is incredible!

We also know that each of us have been created by God as unique from every other person—no two of us are the same. So, your wonderful uniqueness of self is celebrated. But in Romans 12 we are described as being gifted differently from one another, so that we are not to *think too highly of ourselves,* because we all need each other! Each of us brings something valuable to the table, but no one person has the whole package.

The negative use of self is the independent self. Independent from God and even from each other. Self is the root of selfishness. Selfishness and self-centeredness are addressed in this admonition from Paul in Philippians 2:3-4:

> *Let nothing be done through **selfish ambition** or conceit, but in lowliness of mind let each esteem others better than himself. Let each of you look out not only for his own interests, but also for the interests of others.*

We battle with self-centeredness in a myriad of circumstances. We become frustrated or angry when things don't go our way. When we become bored, we seek something exciting or different to stimulate the self. We size up other people in relation to how important they are to ourselves. When we indulge in too much food or drink, we think we owe it to ourselves. These things are evidence of an over-inflated self. In the chapter on sin, we discussed how the *eros* hook works—when we think we have eradicated selfishness, it reappears in another area of our life.

Self is the enemy of our growth into maturity. I still have a self and I can still choose self (overlaps with flesh). I can still choose to live by self's will, wisdom and power. I can walk by self, serve self, follow self, and live under the authority of self. We are admonished to have self-control which again, is the fruit of the Spirit! Without the Spirit's authority and power, self-control from self-effort stimulates independence from God. But remember, fruit grows—it isn't achieved or performed.

Jesus bore us on the cross, and now we have our own cross to bear daily. Reading this should not make us feel condemned but challenged. Not challenged to try harder, but to surrender more. Our victory will never come from our effort to do better—which is rooted in self—but to *choose better*; choosing to surrender our will and ascend into our true being.

PREPOSITIONS HELP US

Since we always have free will to choose, we can still choose self over being filled with the Spirit. Is that different than our old nature? Yes, and it is not just a matter of semantics. Here, prepositions matter! Our old nature as sinner was our identity. We were "out of" Adam. The Greek word *ek* means out of. When you are *ek* of something, that is where you derive your nature or identity. We used to be out of Adam; he was our source. Now we are *ek* of Christ, or out of Him. We have a new source, a new DNA, a new identity. When we were out of Adam, our source dictated who we were and how we would live.

So why is our self-orientation different? Because, we have been given a new nature and our new identity is "the new man" in Christ. We have been reborn as someone new. When we choose to live by self or follow the flesh after being born again, we are neglecting and even betraying our new identity. We have not matured to the point of consistently picking up our cross daily and living by the discipline of being filled with and walking in the Spirit.

What does that look like and how does that happen? Ironically, the biblical picture given to us is through me bearing my own cross—daily! This expression is given to us explicitly in the synoptic gospels (Matthew 10:34-39, Mark 8:32-35, Luke 17:32-34) and implicitly in John's gospel (12:24-26). Though each passage has a slightly different application, each one speaks of "my cross" and bearing it daily.

To bear our cross daily is to remember that through His cross we became a new person with a new nature and a new normal. Some of the old ways we viewed life and interacted with people are not a fit for our new normal. Jesus said that He came to give us life abundantly. The word He used means life that is over and above—more exceeding than anything we've ever known. My life is good, even great, but I don't think I've yet bumped into the ceiling of abundant life! But one thing I understand better than ever is that abundant living comes from abundant dying and dying comes first.

A "fleshly Christian" is a carnal Christian. God's intention for my life is to be a fruitful life because I am abiding in the vine. Abiders are fruit bearers. Now, I am in the vine, but abiding there is a choice I make. I was *saved by the death of Jesus*, but *my life comes from His life*. I was taken out of Adam through His death, but my life is from His resurrected life. The life I now live is His life.

> *Much more then, having now been justified by His blood, we shall be saved from wrath through Him. For if when we were enemies we were reconciled to God through the death of His Son, much more, having been reconciled, we shall be **saved by His life**.* Romans 5:9-10

I say then: Walk in the Spirit, and you shall not fulfill the lust of the flesh. For the flesh lusts against the Spirit, and the Spirit against the flesh; and these are contrary to one another, so that you do not do the things that you wish. But if you are led by the Spirit, you are not under the law. Galatians 5:16-18

Note the order of the answer! *Walk in the Spirit* is first, and it is emphasized. For if we walk in the Spirit, we CANNOT fulfill the desires of the flesh. Many times, people reverse these two. They believe that if they overcome the flesh then they can walk in the Spirit. It doesn't work that way, because though the motives might be good, it is *self* that is trying its best. Self doesn't have enough power.

Therefore, if anyone is in Christ, he is a new creation; old things have passed away; behold, all things have become new. 2 Corinthians 5:17

Any effort to live by the power of self, or out of our flesh—even the desire to do good, will end in failure and frustration:

O wretched man that I am! Who will deliver me from this body of death? I thank God—through Jesus Christ our Lord! So then, with the mind I myself serve the law of God, but with the flesh the law of sin. Romans 7:24,25

How do we sum all this up?

My old identity in Adam died at salvation in the crucifixion of Christ. Who I was in Adam was buried with Him and left in the grave. Our *flesh* and *self* is the manifestation of the life we live independent from God. Fleshly thinking is to think and act under our own authority, on our own, apart from God. It ranges from being overtly rebellious to passively resistant, but it's DNA is independence from God. When we are "in the flesh," or "after the flesh," or acting as self, we are NOT being God conscious or spiritually minded at all. The solution is to *crucify the flesh and to deny self.*

My new nature is my personhood of who God created me to be—fearfully and wonderfully! But it can only find that fulfillment through abiding in Christ, which means that MY cross brings it daily into subjection.

Chapter 10

ME IN CHRIST,
OR CHRIST IN ME?

*Behold, I stand at the door and knock. If anyone
hears My voice and opens the door, I will come in to
him and dine with him, and he with Me.*

REVELATION 3:20

A great memory I have of when God was courting and wooing me during the months leading up to my salvation decision, was of the interactions I had with those who witnessed to me. Of course, it was during the "Jesus Revolution" when lots of young people were coming to faith in Christ, so public witnessing was a common and accepted thing. Not everyone received the message or messengers, but most people politely listened and sometimes they would even jump in the boat! This time of revival in our nation's history is the only real time of revival I have seen or been a part of. What an exciting time it was!

It was also common in 1972 to use tracts. There were two brothers who volunteered for Campus Crusade for Christ who witnessed to me and gave me a tract called *"The Four Spiritual Laws."* They were nice guys, not too pushy, but persistent and faithful. I probably had three or four conversations with them. Though I didn't jump in the boat when we had those conversations, I give them a lot of credit in helping me understand who I was—a lost sinner who needed a personal relationship with Christ.

The primary scripture used to illustrate this invitation from Jesus was Revelation 3:20—*Behold, I stand at the door and knock. If anyone hears My voice and opens the door, I will come in to him and dine with him, and he with Me.*

Though the context for that verse is Jesus speaking to a lampstand church in Laodicea about their risk of losing their passion and becoming lukewarm, it painted a very effective, vivid picture to me, a sinner and lost person who did not have a relationship with God through Jesus.

As these brothers witnessed to me using the tract, *The Four Spiritual Laws*, they described Jesus standing at a door and knocking. The door was to my heart. If I opened the door, He would come into my heart and life and we would have fellowship and more so, begin a personal relationship. It was quite effective. The image of Jesus wanting into MY life—this kind, loving savior knocking on the door of MY heart! But opening the door was up to me. When I did make that decision several months later, that picture of what I was doing and Jesus coming into my life was very real.

So, for a very long time, this was the image I had of a person like me getting saved—Jesus coming into my heart and my life and forgiving me of my sins and of me beginning a personal relationship with Him. But eventually I started noticing not just *Jesus in me* scriptures but *me in Jesus* scriptures. My grid of how we are in relationship with Christ expanded.

What I present here is a more biblically accurate grid of these two pictures of our position in relation to Jesus, though I will always have the best and most grateful memory of Revelation 3:20 and my salvation decision.

US IN CHRIST

In a nutshell, *me in Christ* happens at the moment of my salvation when I am born again. I make a decision to surrender my life to Jesus, and I'm born again! There isn't anything wrong with the picture of Him coming into my life, but it is more accurate to see that when I am saved, I enter into Him—baptized into His death, burial, and resurrection. In that exact moment I became a new person.

Therefore, if anyone is in Christ, he is a new creation; old things have passed away; behold, all things have become new. 2 Corinthians 5:17

So, consider that there is *"all of me in all of Him."* I chose Him and His life for me and everything given to me or done to me and for me is according to the riches of His grace. We have been united to Christ and for every believer, it is the same. I am no more or less forgiven than anyone else. My status as a son is no different than anyone else. For every believer, our identity is the same.

As I am seen from heaven, I am completely new. I have been saved; I have been forgiven; I am a new person; I have been adopted into sonship; I am a living stone in God's house; I am a saint; I have been given the gift of righteousness and have been made righteous; I am sealed in Christ by the Holy Spirit; I have a new Husband; I am complete in Christ; and many other biblical proclamations became true in a split second. Much more has happened than we are aware of! *For in Him dwells all the fullness of the Godhead bodily; and you are* complete *in Him, who is the head of all principality and power.* Colossians 2:9-10

The word for complete is *pleroo*. It means so full that it won't hold anymore. That is how complete we are in Him—to the max. Every believer is made *pleroo* in Christ.

Once again, prepositions matter. Romans 6 is full of the use of the Greek preposition *en*, which means, *"by any place or thing, with the primary idea of rest."* The preposition *with* also describes our union with Christ. For example, look at these two passages:

*What shall we say then? Shall we continue **in** sin that grace may abound? Certainly not! How shall we who died to sin live any longer* *in it? Or do you not know that as many of us as were baptized into Christ Jesus were baptized into His death? Therefore we were buried with Him through baptism into death, that just as Christ was raised from the dead by the glory of the Father, even so we also should walk in newness of life. For if we have been united together in the likeness of His death, certainly we also shall be in the likeness of His resurrection.* Romans 6:1–5

As you therefore have received Christ Jesus the Lord, so walk in Him, rooted and built up in Him and established in the faith, as you have been taught, abounding in it with thanksgiving. Beware lest anyone cheat you through philosophy and empty deceit, according to the tradition of men, according to the basic principles of the world, and not according to Christ. For in Him dwells all the fullness of the Godhead bodily; and you are complete in Him, who is the head of all principality and power. In Him you were also circumcised with the circumcision made without hands, by putting off the body of the sins of the flesh, by the circumcision of Christ, buried with Him in baptism, in which you also were raised with Him through faith in the working of God, who raised Him from the dead. Colossians 2:6–12

Scripture is VERY clear in establishing that our identity is found by being IN and WITH Christ.

CHRIST IN US

Scripture is also pervasive in describing Christ and the Holy Spirit at work in us through the same union. The **Christ in us scriptures**, of which there are many, give us a different aspect of the effect of our salvation.

I begin my new life in Christ as an infant and now I must grow up into a mature version of who I now am. My new life is one of learning to know and understand about my relationship with the

Father, the Son, and the Holy Spirit. I will learn the truth of my new nature and identity and how I have authority over sin, Satan, and this fallen world I live in. I learn that though I am a new creation in Christ, there are times my flesh rises up and wants to take control. I learn how to crucify the flesh and empower the soul by the Spirit to live my life surrendered to Christ.

But all believers are at different levels of spiritual maturity. Unlike *pleroo* where we all are complete in our new identity, we are not all the same in our maturity. A different word for complete that is sometimes translated mature is the word *telios*. *Telios* means to bring something to a complete state. We are all becoming mature at different rates and at different levels in different areas.

The difference between these two words correlates with **in Christ (pleroo)** or **Christ in us (telios).** We are complete, *pleroo* in Christ, but Christ in us (through the Holy Spirit) is helping us grow up and become increasingly more mature, or *telios*.

> *For it is God who **works in you** both to will and to do for His good pleasure.* Philippians 2:13

> *To them God willed to make known what are the riches of the glory of this mystery among the Gentiles: which is **Christ in you, the hope of glory.*** Colossians 1:27

> *My little children, for whom I labor in birth again until Christ is **formed in you**,* Galatians 4:19

> *But we have this treasure in earthen vessels, that the excellence of the power may be of God and not of us.* 2 Corinthians 4:7

In a later chapter on "Abiding in Christ," we will take an in depth look at *Christ in us*.

Both pictures together give us a more complete picture and help to answer many questions. As Major W. Ian Thomas says, *"To be in Christ— that is redemption; but for Christ to be in you, that is sanctification! To be in Christ—that makes you fit for heaven; but for Christ to be in you, that makes you fit for earth! To be in Christ—that changes your destination; but for Christ to be in you changes your destiny!"* [8]

---

8 Thomas, Major W. Ian. (2006). *The Indwelling Life of Christ*, Multomah

Chapter 11

WHAT DO I DO WITH ALL THOSE BIG THEOLOGICAL WORDS?

But the free gift is not like the offense. For if by the one man's offense many died, much more the grace of God and the gift by the grace of the one Man, Jesus Christ, abounded to many. And the gift is not like that which came through the one who sinned. For the judgment which came from one offense resulted in condemnation, but the free gift which came from many offenses resulted in justification. For if by the one man's offense death reigned through the one, much more those who receive abundance of grace and of the gift of righteousness will reign in life through the One, Jesus Christ.)

ROMANS 5:15–17

Golf is a complicated game. More so than many athletic endeavors as there are many moving parts to the golf swing and many different types of shots to hit. Then you have the complexities of golf courses with varying topography, not only for the lie of your ball and your stance but the target, and of course, varying weather conditions. Many moving parts and complex target variables—can anyone simplify this for me? The best golf instructors do that very thing well—they simplify it. The fewer things you have to think of before and during the shot making, the better the results.

So, it is with theology. In trying to answer all the possible questions, the development of Christian doctrine over the span of church history has overcomplicated the simplicity of our faith. One of the results of this complication is the vocabulary of theologians—what they use to make or prove even one facet of the many arguments inherent in theology. We have words like justification, redemption, sanctification, righteousness, restoration, regeneration, and holiness—to name some of them. If we had a good golf instructor that can coach us to simplify the swing, is it possible to simplify theology by looking at and downsizing some of these theological terms? Let's give it a try.

Theologically, what happened at the moment of salvation?

To begin with, we know from scripture that for those who have put their faith in Christ for salvation that we have been justified by the atoning work of Christ through His sacrificial death, burial, and resurrection.

> *Therefore, having been justified by faith, we have peace with God through our Lord Jesus Christ,* Romans 5:1

We are saved by faith in Him and not by works. We are delivered from condemnation and given the gift of justification. We are inheritors of eternal life and heaven is our ultimate destination.

> *Therefore, as through one man's offense judgment came to all men, resulting in condemnation, even so through one Man's righteous act the free gift came to all men, resulting in **justification** of life.* Romans 5:18

I have been regenerated, or, "regened" to have the nature of Christ.

*not by works of righteousness which we have done, **but according to His mercy He saved us**, through the **washing of regeneration** and **renewing of the Holy Spirit**, whom He poured out on us abundantly through Jesus Christ our Savior, that having been **justified** by His grace we should become* *heirs according to the hope of eternal life. This is a faithful saying, and these things I want you to affirm constantly, that those who have believed in God should* **be careful to maintain good works**. *These things are good and profitable to men.* Titus 3:5-8

Note the order—regeneration—*new life and new nature precedes changed behavior*, called good works in this passage. I am a new genetic spiritual being! How did that come about? Through my new birth into my new life *preceded* by my death out of my old life.

My new birth was from a new seed.

> *Since you have purified your souls* **in obeying the truth through the Spirit** *in sincere love of the brethren, love one another fervently with a pure heart,* **having been born again, not of corruptible seed but incorruptible***, through the word of God which lives and abides forever,* 1 Peter 1:22-23

I have been born again of incorruptible seed—the seed of Christ—I am no longer of the seed of Adam. My very nature was changed, through death and through being raised up. When I make a choice now to do something through self, apart from God, I will fail. That is what self does. But my new being is empowered through the Spirit to choose Him and His way for my life—moment by moment, day by day, until arriving as a mature version of my new man.

> *till we all come to the unity of the faith and of the knowledge of the Son of God, to a perfect man, to the measure of the stature of the fullness of Christ; that we should no longer be children, tossed to and fro and carried about with every wind of doctrine, by the trickery of men, in the cunning craftiness of deceitful plotting, but, speaking the truth in love,* **may grow up in all things** *into Him who is the head—Christ.* Ephesians 4:13-15

Already and not yet—how can that be?

When does life begin, at conception or sometime during one of the trimesters? This is debated all the time in society and especially since the recent overturn of Roe vs Wade and the return of the abortion decision to the states. But I believe life begins at conception.

We have some good friends that struggled with infertility. Eventually, they went through a process of using a surrogate mother to conceive their egg and sperm. They told me they were in the hospital with the doctor when the fertilization took place. They asked the doctor if there was a way to know if it was successful. "Oh yes," the doctor said, "you will see a flash of light." As they watched the process on a screen, sure enough, they saw the flash of light! Their son is now a thriving teenager!

Sometime around nine months prior to September 5, 1953, my mom and dad conceived me. In a flash of a moment, sperm joined with an egg, and I began. God held me for nine months before I was held by my mom or dad. He fashioned me and made me. Psalm 139:13-16 describes us being made by God in our mother's womb. Eight different Hebrew words are used to describe this miracle. The first of those words means that we were made to belong to God. We are His intended possession, first and foremost above all else! But it also says that I was fearfully and wonderfully made by Him. *I began with a flash of light. So did you*!

The story I have already talked about in my salvation journey, I tell again in this context. For eighteen and a half years I was apart from God until I decided to choose to be chosen—until I gave my life to Christ. Immediately, I was justified and regenerated and given eternal life. Eternal life started at the moment of salvation—not someday in the future when I depart this earth. When I was first saved, I was an infant version of this new creation that will grow up to look more and more like Him. I am already, and still becoming who that new man is!

So, let's look at three important biblical words found in many scriptures that talk about us—*righteousness, holiness,* and *sanctification*. These three words explain us as *already and becoming*.

A sermon preached by Clark Whitten many years ago is a favorite. The subject of the message was "God can't live in a dirty house, but He lives in you!" What is the implication of that statement? That we aren't dirty! We've been made clean, holy, righteous, and sanctified. But aren't there scriptures that say that we are still becoming sanctified and that we are to pursue holiness? Of course, the answer is yes! We are already sanctified, and we are becoming sanctified.

RIGHTEOUSNESS

Paul, in Romans 5 tells us two things about our righteousness. It is a GIFT given to us. But also, we have been MADE righteous.

> *For if by the one man's offense death reigned through the one, much more those who receive abundance of grace and of the **gift of righteousness** will reign in life through the One, Jesus Christ.)* Romans 5:17

> *For as by one man's disobedience many were made sinners, so also by one Man's obedience many will be **made righteous**.* Romans 5:19

What is righteousness? What does the word mean? The word *dikasiosune*, or one of its derivatives, is translated as *righteous* in many scriptures. It means *that which is just*. Righteousness fulfills the claims of another, which in a believer's case, is God. To be righteous, we conform to the claims of God, so that we have right standing with Him.

But we know that we can't perform in our own behavior to meet those claims, so in place of our own righteousness, we have been given the gift of Jesus's own righteousness. Jesus is the only person who ever lived a perfect life. It has been given to us as a gift, not earned. It was imputed to us. We are in relationship with God not through our own righteousness, but His.

Furthermore, we have been made righteous (v. 19). The word *made* is *kathistemi*, which means *to be set, to stand, to cause to be, to become*. We are righteous with His righteousness. God looks upon us and sees that we are righteous with Jesus's righteousness. We are fit vessels to be the temple of the Holy Spirit. God lives inside of us.

What about when we mess up? Doesn't that make us dirty again? We may feel dirty and certainly we need to interact with God about what we have done. We need to be able to experience God's grace, get His mind and truth about our failure, and be healed and set free and move forward. But even in our failure we still have the righteousness of Christ. It is always His righteousness. If our own behavior could make us righteous, we never needed a savior in the first place.

The more I mature in Christ, the more my life becomes conformed to the righteous life of Christ. *I am already and I am becoming.*

SANCTIFICATION

For many years, I was told that I was justified at the moment of salvation but that my sanctification is ongoing and progressive for the rest of my life. When I taught new believers basic discipleship principles, this is what I told them. This is partly true and partly wrong. A review of scriptures shows that we are *already sanctified, but also becoming*. Let's first look at the definitions.

Sanctification—hagiasmos—this word is sometimes translated as *holiness*—separation unto God.

Sanctification of the Holy Spirit is produced by the Holy Spirit—"*it refers not only to the activity of the Holy Spirit in setting man apart unto salvation and transferring him into the ranks of the redeemed, but also to enabling him to be holy even as God is holy.*"Zodhiates

The definition of the word *sanctified—hagiazo*—to make holy; to make clean, render pure; to consecrate, devote, set apart; to regard and venerate as holy.

As we looked at the word righteousness and now at sanctification, we see similar meaning between these words in the family of "redemption" words. These words all point to a radical change of "newness" that is both already and becoming. The "already" happens at the point of new birth. Staying with our theme of growing up, when we receive our new DNA, it is as an infant. Babies must grow up. So, we are already, but to grow up into our "new man," to become a mature adult version of who we became in our new birth, we must not stay in infant form. Growing up requires something on our part. Here are some sample scriptures that delineate already, and not yet.

ALREADY SANCTIFIED (PAST TENSE)

To the church of God which is at Corinth, to those who are sanctified in Christ Jesus, called to be saints, with all who in every place call on the name of Jesus Christ our Lord, both theirs and ours. 1 Corinthians 1:2

And such were some of you. But you were washed, but you were sanctified, but you were justified in the name of the Lord Jesus and by the Spirit of our God. 1 Corinthians 6:11

For by one offering He has perfected forever those who are being sanctified. Hebrews 10:14

BECOMING SANCTIFIED

I speak in human terms because of the weakness of your flesh. For just as you presented your members as slaves of uncleanness, and of lawlessness leading to more lawlessness, so now present your members as slaves of righteousness for holiness. Romans 6:19

For you know what commandments we gave you through the Lord Jesus. For this is the will of God, your sanctification: that you should abstain from sexual immorality; that each of you should know how to possess his own vessel in sanctification and honor, not in passion of lust, like the Gentiles who do not know God; 1 Thessalonians 4:2–5

Therefore if anyone cleanses himself from the latter, he will be a vessel for honor, sanctified and useful for the Master, prepared for every good work. 2 Timothy 2:21

Let's move on to *holiness*, another word that shows that we are already, but also becoming.

HOLY/HOLINESS

Following the same pattern and scripture contexts, we already are holy and encouraged to pursue holiness. First, the definition—

Holy—hagios—set apart, sanctified, consecrated—as in the saints. It comes from a common root, *hagnos*, meaning chaste, pure. Its primary idea is separation, consecration, devotion to the service of God, sharing in God's purity and abstaining from earth's defilement.

Like the word righteousness, to be holy, or to attain the state or condition of holiness can refer either to "being made" holy, or it can describe our new normal quality of life, based on our choices. In other words, we have both been *made holy* and we are to *live a holy life* by the quality of life we choose, *because we are able to!* We see the distinction below.

MADE holy—The state of holiness that has been given to us, that we have through our identity in Christ:

In the body of His flesh through death, to present you holy, and blameless, and above reproach in his sight—Colossians 1:22

Therefore, as the elect of God, holy and beloved, put on tender mercies, kindness, humility, meekness, longsuffering—Colossians 3:12

If anyone defiles the temple of God, God will destroy him. For the temple of God is holy, which temple you are. 1 Corinthians 3:17

BECOMING or pursuing holiness—The state of holiness that is reflected from choices we make—our new normal—because we have been made holy, we can choose holiness.

Therefore, having these promises, beloved, let us cleanse ourselves from all filthiness of the flesh and spirit, perfecting holiness in the fear of God. 2 Corinthians 7:1

For they indeed for a few days chastened us as seemed best to them, but He for our profit, that we may be partakers of His holiness. Hebrews 12:10

but as He who called you is holy, you also be holy in all your conduct, because it is written, "Be holy, for I am holy." 1 Peter 1:15–16

We are encouraged and even commanded to pursue holiness. It is incumbent on us to desire God's highest and best. We make choices all the time. Here are some reasons to pursue holiness:

- Fulfill God's deepest purposes and desires for my life— it's who I am.
- Deny Satan's access.
- Deeper intimacy with God.
- Joy and peace.
- Relationships with other people.
- It would be a betrayal to myself and others not to.

We have the power to live a holy life! Believing what the word says about us, we can live a holy life because we have been made new. Our new spiritual DNA makes this our new normal. *We don't become holy because we live holy, we live holy because we have been made holy!*

Our new spiritual DNA is:
- A new identity as a new creation in Christ
- A new nature—as a partaker of the divine nature
- The resurrection power of the Holy Spirit—He works in me
- The authority and power of His word
- The dynamic of being united with Christ

Therefore gird up the loins of your mind, be sober, and rest your hope fully upon the grace that is to be brought to you at the revelation of Jesus Christ; as obedient children, not conforming yourselves to the former lusts, as in your ignorance; but as He who called you is holy, you also be holy in all your conduct, because it is written, "Be holy, for I am holy." 1 Peter 1:13–16

Grace and peace be multiplied to you in the knowledge of God and of Jesus our Lord, as His divine power has given to us all things that pertain to life and godliness, through the knowledge of Him who called us by glory and virtue, by which have been given to us exceedingly great and precious promises, that through these you may be partakers of the divine nature, having escaped the corruption that is in the world through lust. 2 Peter 1:2-4

Chapter 12
HOW DO I RELATE TO THE LAW?

For I through the law died to the law that I might live to
God. I have been crucified with Christ; it is no longer I who
live, but Christ lives in me; and the life which I now live in
the flesh I live by faith in the Son of God, who loved me and
gave Himself for me. I do not set aside the grace of God; for if
righteousness comes through the law, then Christ died in vain.
GALATIANS 2:19–21

What is the first thing you do when you pass a police patrol car? You look down to see your speed limit, of course! And then you sigh with relief, or you keep watching in your mirror to see if the policeman is turning around. We all know the drill. Those laws are in place for a reason, and scripture encourages us to honor those in civil authority over us as they are there for our good.

What about the Mosaic law, also known as the Rabbinic law—the oral law that was prevalent at the time of Christ and still is today? Jesus said He didn't come to do away with it, but that He would fulfill it. To say that there is no law or to be against the law is called *antinomianism*, which is the same as lawlessness. None of us want to live in that kind of society.

There are varied opinions and beliefs about our relationship to the Mosaic law, so there is no pretending that the answers given here are considered universal or perhaps even widely agreed with. We are helped by a number of scriptures and a wonderful metaphor from Romans chapter 7. So let us start with some statements in general that are based on scripture.

- We are not under law, but under grace . Romans 6:14
- The law was given to Moses so that the people of Israel would be differentiated from the nations and a light to them. Genesis 22:18, Leviticus 20:26
- The law is a tutor, to bring us to Christ. Galatians 3:24
- The law is our former husband. Romans 7:5-6
- The law reflects the nature and character of God. Romans 7:12
- The law reveals the nature of sin and the nature of the sinner. Romans 7:7-9
- The law imputes sin—without the law, sin is dead. Romans 7:10-12, Romans 5:12-14
- We are saved not by works but by grace through faith. Ephesians 2:8-9

Of course, these statements don't answer all the questions about our relationship to the law, or everyone would agree. So, what questions might we have?

If I am saved by grace through faith, does the law mean anything to me anymore? What meaning and value does the law have to me now?

Yes, it does! The law helps us understand the character and nature of God. It teaches us about holiness and the distinction between the creator and the creation.

Is the law still something to be obeyed?

We don't keep the law to be justified before God or to attain a stature of righteousness. However, the New Testament is full of admonitions and instructions that exemplify the newness of life and our behavior as a new creation in Christ. Examples of these admonitions are; *"consider one another as more important than ourselves; walk in a manner worthy of the calling with which you have been called; let all bitterness and anger and clamor and slander be put away from you; put on the new self and lay aside the old self; devote yourselves to prayer, keeping alert in it with an attitude of thanksgiving."*

What does it mean in the New Covenant that the laws of God are now written on our hearts?

Ezekiel 36:26-27 describes the new heart we receive in the New Covenant. Because we love God and people with a new heart, we find a "new natural" for us. To have this new heart means we have the *capacity* to love people as God loves them, with *agape* love. But we are also enjoined in many scriptures to "put away" fleshly thoughts and behaviors that are contrary to who we now are. Perhaps we could say the Torah (instruction for how to live) in the New Covenant exemplifies how God's people with a new heart are to live.

Several times Jesus emphasized our obedience to Him. What does He mean by that?

We relate to Jesus in many ways. He is our savior, healer, redeemer, and deliverer. But He is also Lord, and we are under His authority in all things. He spoke of us keeping His commandments and that *"if we love Him we will obey Him."*

When Jesus was asked what the greatest commandment is, He Answered:

Then one of them, a lawyer, asked Him a question, testing Him, and saying, "Teacher, which is the great commandment in the law?"

Jesus said to him, "You shall love the LORD your God with all your heart, with all your soul, and with all your mind. This is the first and great commandment. And the second is like it: You shall love your neighbor as yourself. **On these two commandments hang all the Law and the Prophets.** *Matthew 22:35-40*

It can be argued that these two commands encompass any of the Mosaic law that affect our relationship to God and to other people. Other parts of the mosaic law were given for purposes that apply to that time and culture, such as the dietary and ceremonial laws.

But obedience to Christ goes beyond commands in scripture. We all pray concerning decisions we are making. Why would we pray unless we believe that God cares and that He will lead and guide us? Obedience to Christ in daily living brings us peace, joy, and fruitfulness.

How does the Bible describe the law to us as believers?

The law is *holy, just, and good,* and the law *imputes sin.*

What shall we say then? Is the law sin? Certainly not! On the contrary, I would not have known sin except through the law. For I would not have known covetousness unless the law had said, "You shall not covet." **But sin, taking opportunity by the commandment, produced in me all manner of evil desire. For apart from the law sin was dead.** *I was alive once without the law, but when the commandment came, sin revived and I died. And the commandment, which was to bring life, I found to bring death.1 For sin, taking occasion by the commandment, deceived me, and by it killed me.* **Therefore the law is holy, and the commandment holy and just and good.** *Romans 7:7-12*

Or do you not know, brethren (for I speak to those who know the *law), that the law has dominion over a man as long as he lives? For the woman who has a husband is bound by the law to her husband as long as he lives. But if the husband dies, she is released from the law of her husband. So then if, while her husband lives, she marries another man, she will be called an adulteress; but if her husband dies, she is free from that law, so that she is no adulteress, though she has married another man. Therefore, my brethren, you also have become dead to the law through the body of Christ, that you may be married to another—to Him who was raised from the dead, that we should bear fruit to God. **For when we were in the flesh, the sinful passions which were aroused by the law were at work in our members to bear fruit to death.** But now we have been delivered from the law, having died to what we were held by, so that **we should serve in the newness of the Spirit and not in the oldness of the letter.** Romans 7:1-6*

What does it mean that Jesus did not come to abolish the law but to fulfill it?

Jesus kept the law perfectly, as God always intended it. Jesus, who knew the Father intimately, knew the heart of God which transcends any code of written law. He didn't abolish it as it remains. The law will never die nor pass away.

For assuredly, I say to you, till heaven and earth pass away, one jot or one tittle will by no means pass from the law till all is fulfilled. Matthew 5:18

As long as the law serves its purpose as a tutor to bring people to Christ, it has not yet been fulfilled.

Jesus's *Sermon on the Mount* set up a confrontation between the **Pharisaic application of the law, God's original intent of the law, and Jesus's fulfillment of the law.** The development of the oral law traditions for hundreds of years before Jesus's ministry resulted in a heavy accumulation of legal interpretations in order to keep people within the boundaries of the Torah. If the Torah was a fence for people to live within to live a certain life, then the traditions were an attempt to make the fence much higher to safeguard against people violating the Torah.

For example, the law in Deuteronomy 14 that says, *"You shall not boil a young goat in its mother's milk,"* was probably intended to counteract a practice by some pagan groups in that day and time. But it evolved to the application of not eating meat and dairy together which expanded to elaborate rabbinic rules about cooking utensils being separated, the length of time between dairy and meat for digestion, etc. Interestingly, a few verses before this law is this verse in Deuteronomy 12:32 that says, *"Whatever I command you, be careful to observe it; you shall not add to it nor take away from it."*

But add to it they did! Rabbinic Judaism believes Moses was given all of the oral law and traditions as well as the 613 commands in the Torah, so it is all authoritative. In the Sermon on the Mount, Jesus gave several examples, saying, "You have heard it said", or "It is written—but I say to you," and then He raised the bar. We find an example in Matthew 5:21-22:

> *You have heard that it was said to those of old, 'You shall not murder, and whoever murders will be in danger of the judgment.' But I say to you that whoever is angry with his brother without a cause shall be in danger of the judgment. And whoever says to his brother, 'Raca!' shall be in danger of the council. But whoever says, 'You fool!' shall be in danger of hell fire.*

Jesus's statements about the law superseded the Pharisaic teaching of the law. The one who said, *"For I say to you, that unless your righteousness exceeds the righteousness of the scribes and Pharisees, you will by no means enter the kingdom of heaven* [9]*" also said, "Come to Me, all you who labor and are heavy laden, and I will give you rest. Take My yoke upon you and learn from Me, for I am gentle and lowly in heart, and you will find rest for your souls. For My yoke is easy and My burden is light."* [10]

What are we to make of all of this? Jesus raised the bar from behavior to thoughts and attitudes as well, so He could convincingly make the case that no one could attain righteousness through keeping the law. We all fail. We are all lawbreakers. Therefore, to attain righteousness, it must come another way and He is the way. The law, as righteous and holy and good as it is, was never meant to be kept by us to attain righteousness. And the law itself has no power to enable us to keep it. But it does have the authority to judge and condemn us.

Jesus raised the law to its original intent—to make us lawbreakers so that *everyone* would need a Savior—someone who would keep the law for us when we fail. We are in covenant with God because we are in Christ, the one who fulfills the demands of the Covenant. Christ lives His life in me and through me. Now, when I live righteously, it is Christ living in me.

Yes, the law is holy and righteous and good. I agree with the psalmist who said:

> *How can a young man cleanse his way? By taking heed according to Your word. With my whole heart I have sought You; Oh, let me not wander from Your commandments! Your word I have hidden in my heart, That I might not sin against You. Blessed are You, O Lord! Teach me Your statutes. With my lips I have declared All the judgments of Your mouth. I have rejoiced in the way of Your testimonies, as much as in all riches. I will meditate on Your precepts and contemplate Your ways. I will delight myself in Your statutes; I will not forget Your word."* Psalm 119:9–16

9 Matthew 5:20
10 Matthew 11:28-30

Chapter 13

IS THERE SUCH A THING AS CHEAP GRACE?

Likewise you also, reckon yourselves to be dead indeed to sin, but
alive to God in Christ Jesus our Lord. Therefore do not let sin reign
in your mortal body, that you should obey it in its lusts. And do not
present your members as instruments of unrighteousness to sin but
present yourselves to God as being alive from the dead, and your
members as instruments of righteousness to God. For sin shall not
have dominion over you, for you are not under law but under grace.
ROMANS 6:11–14

Cheap grace. What a statement. In context, when you hear the accusation that a church teaches cheap grace or that a person believes in cheap grace, they are really saying that a person is using forgiveness as a license to live any way they want to. In other words, they are addressing irresponsible living. But in my opinion, that is what they should call it. The words cheap and grace should never be spoken together. To call grace cheap is a horrendous and offensive misstatement. There is nothing cheap about it—neither from the standpoint of what it cost God to provide it or what it costs us to receive it and live it. So, let's address the core issue of irresponsible living and get the right perspective.

Jesus died for our sins 2000 years ago. The sins He died for made clean the previous sins of those who had preceded Him in death, when "He led captivity captive" and took those Old Testament men and women of faith to heaven with Him. He also died for the sins that had been committed by His followers. But all other sins He died for were in the future, including yours and mine. When we came to faith in Christ, His shed blood cleansed us of our sins. Which ones? All of them—past, present, and future. His once and forever and perfect sacrifice will not be repeated.

So how do we obtain this forgiveness and this cleansing? By trusting in Him and His finished work for our salvation—not in our own works.

For by grace you have been saved through faith, and that not of yourselves; it is the gift of God, not of works, lest anyone should boast. Ephesians 2:8-9

Some Christians have no trouble believing that at salvation all their previous sins are forgiven by grace, but to *stay saved* requires obedient living, or works. Don't turn me off yet—hang with me. I will soon address irresponsible living. But first, we must see the fallacy that staying saved is performance-based. If moral perfection couldn't obtain right standing with God, then moral imperfection can't disqualify our right standing with God. We are in right standing with God because we have been given Jesus's righteousness. The same gift of grace that cleansed me of my sins continually cleanses me of my sins—all of them and for all time!

For by one offering He has perfected forever those who are being sanctified. Hebrews 10:14

Note the flow of that incredible verse and personalize it. He has *perfected forever*, YOU, even though you are *being* sanctified. We discussed in a previous chapter that we are already sanctified *and* are being sanctified. This is an incredible truth for those who have truly been born again. I will say something controversial here. There are people who have responded to salvation opportunities for one reason—to get a ticket to heaven. God knows who they are. We don't. There is no surrender of their life. There is no real confession and repentance. There is no real encounter with God. There is only a response to a message and an invitation and a desire for a business transaction with God that gives them a place in heaven. They haven't been born again. They are still unregenerated and the sad truth is they may not know it.

For those who are born again, there are many things that happened at salvation that they only become knowledgeable of over time. That is a purpose of this book! I will say it again, salvation is the beginning of all things new, but it is not the end of sin in our life. It IS the end of **sin's dominion** in our life—if we live according to the truth of our new identity. Remember your identity—you are not a sinner saved by grace but a saint who sometimes sins!

Grace is not a license to sin. Paul asked and answered that question two times emphatically in Romans chapter 6:

> *What shall we say then? Shall we continue in sin that grace may abound?* **Certainly not!** *How shall we who died to sin live any longer in it?* Romans 6:1–2

> *What then? Shall we sin because we are not under law but under grace? Certainly not! Do you not know that to whom you present yourselves slaves to obey, you are that one's slaves whom you obey, whether of sin leading to death, or of obedience leading to righteousness?* Romans 6:15–17

I will say it again—grace is not a license to sin! Knowing that I am forgiven even before I sin is not a license to sin. To believe that God's forgiveness gives me a license to sin completely misunderstands the DNA of grace and its power. Rightly understood, grace *disempowers* sin and empowers dominion over sin. In fact, let's shift the emphasis from sinning to not sinning. Instead of, "Why do I sin?" let's ask, "Why am I not sinning?" That's a fun one to answer.

I love to refresh myself in the truth about who I am and why I have victory over sin. Does that mean that I never sin? By no means—as 1 John says, *"if we say we have no sin, the truth is not in us."* But as a new creation in Christ, as one whose body of sin was crucified and buried, my new normal is to live in victory over sin. When I see myself as what the Bible calls me, *a saint*, I see myself as one who has been exchanged from who I used to be. And if I believe it, I am empowered to live as my new normal. This isn't some kind of voodoo mind game or a manipulation of words. It is the power of truth!

When parents give a blessing to their children consistently and repeatedly over time with words of affirmation, children come to believe these words and live according to them. Sadly, the opposite is also true. I challenge you to read through the New Testament and look for yourself. You are all throughout the scriptures. Write down what it says. You will not only be amazed to read these words of affirmation, but you will also start to believe them and live them!

No, grace is not cheap. It cost God the death of His son. Yes, He was resurrected, but we cannot imagine what the sinless Jesus endured when He was made to be sin for us on the cross during those three hours of darkness. And grace is not cheap for us either. It is free, we don't earn it—but it costs us everything we are and have. In Matthew, Mark and Luke, Jesus exhorts us to take up our cross daily—our own personal cross. In that day when He spoke those words, you would never find someone wearing a cross as a piece of jewelry. The cross was an instrument of death, and it was feared and despised, but Jesus told us to take it up daily.

> James Fowler says, *"At the same time, be advised, for to accept God's grace will cost you everything. God's grace is not the "cheap grace" of a free ride, but the "costly grace" that cost Jesus His life and will cost you yours as well."* [11]

---

11 Fowler, James. (2005). *Christ at Work in You*, CIY Publishing

It is our cross, personalized to us, and it tells us that life in Christ is a life of *obedience* and *freedom* and *power*. Note these three words together!

There are consequences for sin. Consequences can include reaping what we sow, damage to relationships, compromises to our physical and emotional health, financial damage, emotional instability, and many other things. Each of us can tell stories of self-imposed problems after we came to faith. They can even include God's pruning and discipline. But consequences do not include God's condemnation and wrath.

The exchanged life we now have cost us the life we used to have. Our "all in" decision resulted in a great exchange. We are exhorted in Ephesians to take off who we used to be and put on who we are now:

> *That you put off, concerning your former conduct, the old man which grows corrupt according to the deceitful lusts, and be renewed in the spirit of your mind, and that you put on the new man which was created according to God, in true righteousness and holiness.*
> Ephesians 4: 22–24

The hinge between taking off the old man and putting on the new man is *being renewed in the spirit of our mind*. The metaphor of taking off and putting on is like a garment—exchanging a new garment for an old one. The old one doesn't fit any more. It doesn't look right, or feel right, or smell right. It isn't right and can't be right because it is no longer us. Our license to sin was done away with when we were born again.

Rightly understanding the power of grace frees us from the power of sin. Grace is not cheap. If someone intentionally sins because of forgiveness, they haven't cheapened grace because it can't be cheapened. They are just acting foolishly.

Chapter 14
HOW ETERNAL IS ETERNAL LIFE?

In Him we have redemption through His blood, the forgiveness of sins, according to the riches of His grace which He made to abound toward us in all wisdom and prudence, having made known to us the mystery of His will, according to His good pleasure which He purposed in Himself, that in the dispensation of the fullness of the times He might gather together in one all things in Christ, both which are in heaven and which are on earth—in Him. In Him also we have obtained an inheritance, being predestined according to the purpose of Him who works all things according to the counsel of His will, that we who first trusted in Christ should be to the praise of His glory. In Him you also trusted, after you heard the word of truth, the gospel of your salvation; in whom also, having believed, you were sealed with the Holy Spirit of promise, who is the guarantee of our inheritance until the redemption of the purchased possession, to the praise of His glory.
EPHESIANS 1:7–14

One of my favorite bosses was my cousin Clarence. Clarence was a soft spoken, hardworking, talented supervisor in my dad's meat packing plant. He ran the "sausage kitchen," where all the sausage products were made. He was good at his job and a good man to work for.

But Clarence was bound up with some unhealthy thinking and even with all my logical persuasion he couldn't be convinced differently. He believed there was no way this side of heaven to know whether he would be admitted to heaven until after he died. I know there are denominations that teach this, and he learned it somewhere. But without any assurance of salvation, he lived with an uncertainty that inspired a works/performance based transactional relationship with God. Though I was a very young Christian at the time and unlearned in the scriptures, I couldn't accept Clarence's view.

Years later, when I developed a personal theology, I believed that I could have assurance of my salvation. *But I also believed I could lose it through rejecting Christ with the same free will from which I chose to accept Him.* I held that view for a long time and taught it in discipling other believers. The issue of how eternal is eternal life is one of the most debated theological questions in the New Testament era of the past two thousand years. Once saved, can I lose my salvation?

I remember debating this question with a Baptist pastor friend of mine. The challenge I posed to him was that we all know people who were professed believers who had "fallen away" from the faith either through sin or unbelief, or both. They no longer believed. Indeed, a contemporary trend among some long-time believers are those who have gone through a "deconstruction" of their beliefs. They have reexamined long held beliefs about the authority of scripture, the resurrection of Christ, and other core beliefs and in some cases have rejected their beliefs and exchanged them for a different belief system. Alisa Childers, in her excellent book, *"Another Gospel,"* tells of her own journey through deconstruction, though in her case she came back to an even more solid confirmation of her faith.

There are scriptural warnings against members of local congregations being led astray by deceiving doctrines. The battle against heresy was waged and fought by leaders of the early church and by the early apostolic fathers. The development of Christian doctrine in the early centuries of the church is in response to the many heretical efforts to deceive and destroy our scriptural foundations. This is not a new problem—it's been around since Pentecost. And today the battle continues.

But my pastor friend had a short answer for those people I described that had "fallen away." He said that they were never really saved to begin with. This scripture seems to support his view:

> *They went out from us, but they were not of us; for if they had been of us, they would have continued with us; but they went out that they might be made manifest, that none of them were of us.* 1 John 2:19

My friend's version of eternal security stayed in the back of my mind. I neither accepted it or rejected it, but I catalogued it as something I wasn't sure about. However, my personal grace journey enabled me to start seeing something I hadn't seen before. I saw a pattern in the word pictures that describe us coming into union with Christ in salvation. It is the word pictures and the pattern that we will now look at.

The pattern is fourfold:
- God does it—we cannot do it for ourselves.
- It is thorough and complete—nothing is left undone.
- The *me* becomes *we*—though it is a personal salvation experience, it is also into the community of believers, the Church.
- He who did it is the only one who can undo it—I can't, and He won't!

In the following word pictures, notice the fourfold pattern for each of them:

1. **I have been born anew into Christ.**
   Having been born again, not of corruptible seed but incorruptible, through the word of God which lives and abides forever—1 Peter 1:23

Jesus told Nicodemus that one must be born of water AND the Spirit to enter the Kingdom of God. Spiritually reborn. What is that? Birth of course represents the beginning of something new. We all come into this world naturally out of our mother's womb. God breathed life into us at conception and in the womb, God held us and made us, putting in what we would need to fulfill His plan and purpose for us. All of that is activated when we accept Christ and are born again.

Every person has a story to tell of the events and circumstances leading up to their decision to surrender their life to Christ. Everyone's story is different, but the common denominator is God's involvement in the process of wooing or drawing us. We don't "find" God on our own or stumble over Him accidentally. This wooing time is analogous to the time we were in our mother's womb prior to our physical birth. It is as though we are in a spiritual womb until the day we are born again. The new birth is of the Spirit, just as Jesus explained to Nicodemus.

We are born again as an infant version of who we are becoming, and we definitely have to grow up. One should not stay as an infant! But the DNA of who we are as a new creation is all there. Nothing is left out. And immediately at our new birth we become part of Christian community. Our salvation experience is very individualized between us and Jesus, but the me becomes we. We always retain our personal relationship, but we also grow in that relationship in both a personal and community context. We are not meant to be alone.

And finally, how do you "unborn" yourself? Why do we think we can undo something we couldn't do on our own in the first place?

2. **I have been *baptized* into Christ.**

   Or do you not know that as many of us as were baptized into Christ Jesus were baptized Into His death? Therefore we were buried with Him through baptism into death, that just as Christ was raised from the dead by the glory of the Father, even so we also should walk in newness of life.
   Romans 6:3,4

This word picture from Romans 6 is one of TOTAL identification and inclusion with the death, burial, and resurrection of Christ. The very nature of baptism, *baptizo*, means to be immersed into something until a transformation takes place of the immersed object—as in a cloth being dyed a different color, or a cucumber becoming a pickle! It is a total transformation. A pickle can never be a cucumber again.

Who is the baptizer? The Holy Spirit, and the Spirit baptizes us into Christ for our personal salvation experience but also into the body of Christ, the church. The *me* becomes *we*.

For by one Spirit we were all baptized into one body—whether Jews or Greeks, whether slaves or free—and have all been made to drink into one Spirit. For in fact the body is not one member but many—1 Corinthians 12:13,14. We are not alone!

Do we think we can unbaptize ourselves? We can mess up and act like cucumbers, but we are still pickles!

3. **I have been *adopted into* sonship.**
    But when the fullness of the time had come, God sent forth His Son, born of a woman, born under the law, to redeem those who were under the law, that we might receive the adoption as sons. And because you are sons, God has sent forth the Spirit of His Son into your hearts, crying out, "Abba, Father!" Therefore you are no longer a slave but a son, and if a son, then an heir of God through Christ. Galatians 4:4-7

In Chapter 5 we learned about the process of Roman adoption. Here are the key facts—it is initiated by the adopting father; it is a permanent, irrevocable, legal act; and the son takes on a completely new identity with all the rights that go with it. We can't adopt ourselves into God's family—He must do it. At the time of adoption, though it is an individual act, we become part of a family.

4. **I have been *transferred into* the Kingdom of His Son.**

He has delivered us from the power of darkness and conveyed us into the kingdom of the Son of His love, Colossians 1:13

This wonderful picture also speaks of total transformation. We are moved by Him, delivered, and conveyed to a totally different kingdom. From darkness to light, law to grace, bondage to freedom, death to life, Adam to Christ. Since we don't move ourselves, why would we think we have the power to move ourselves back? And the Kingdom of the Son is populated with many just like us.

5. **I have been *married* in.**

Or do you not know, brethren (for I speak to those who know the law), that the law has dominion over a man as long as he lives? For the woman who has a husband is bound by the law to her husband as long as he lives. But if the husband dies, she is released from the law of her husband. So then if, while her husband lives, she marries another man, she will be called an adulteress; but if her husband dies, she is free from that law, so that she is no adulteress, though she has married another man. Therefore, my brethren, you also have become dead to the law through the body of Christ, that you may be married to another—to Him who was raised from the dead, that we should bear fruit to God. Romans 7:1-4

As we saw in chapter 12, our only way out of an impossible marriage is through death. Married to the law, we had a moral husband who was impossible to please. He was demanding and could not be satisfied, and we were reminded of our failures continually. And he could do nothing to empower us to live according to his standards. The only way out of this marriage is through death. Since he isn't going to die, we had to die, in order to be married to our new husband, Christ. Christ is perfect in His demands, and He empowers us to live His life. When we fail, He meets His own demands and closes the gap even when we don't.

We are joined to our new husband as the church. The *me* becomes *we*. Will Christ divorce us? May it never be! Not even when we fail!

6. **I have been *circumcised* in.**

In Him you were also circumcised with the circumcision made without hands, by putting off the body of the sins of the flesh, by the circumcision of Christ, buried with Him in baptism, in which you also were raised with Him through faith in the working of God, who raised Him from the dead. And you, being dead in your trespasses and the uncircumcision of your flesh, He has made alive together with Him, having forgiven you all trespasses, having wiped out the handwriting of requirements that was against us, which was contrary to us. And He has taken it out of the way, having nailed it to the cross. Colossians 2:11-14

Two profound truths are given in this passage. One concerns the circumcision of Christ; the other is our circumcision. Neither is talking about physical circumcision but a spiritual event.

What is the *circumcision of Christ* as a spiritual event? I believe the answer is found in this scripture*:*

For He made Him who knew no sin to be sin for us, that we might become the righteousness of God in Him, 2 Corinthians 5:21

Since the circumcised foreskin is a piece of flesh and is likened to the "body of sin," Jesus took on not just the penalty for our sins on the cross, but the "body of sin," the nature of Adam. This is how he takes the power of sin through death and into the grave so that when we are baptized into Him, *we are also circumcised into Him.*

Just as we were made to totally identify with Christ through baptism, so also through circumcision. Our "body of sin" has been sent to the grave. We don't circumcise ourselves, God does it as part of our miraculous new birth. And it is permanent. *Foreskins don't grow back!*

7. **I have been *built in*.**

   In whom you also are being built together for a dwelling place of God in the Spirit. Ephesians 2:22

Here, and in 1 Peter 2:5, where we are described as living stones, we find ourselves in a Temple context. You and I are individually the Temple of the Holy Spirit,[12] and for us to be the dwelling place of the Spirit, we have been made holy and sanctified and clean. The Holy Spirit doesn't move in and out. Unlike in the Old Testament, his dwelling is constant and permanent. He is purposeful in every area of our life. He is at work in us to teach, guide, empower, counsel, and comfort us.

Corporately, each local church is the Temple of the Holy Spirit as well. [13] The *me* has become *we*, and God is not going to tear down or remove living stones who are a part of His dwelling.

8. **I have been *carried in*.**

   What man of you, having a hundred sheep, if he loses one of them, does not leave the ninety-nine in the wilderness, and go after the one which is lost until he finds it? And when he has found it, he lays it on his shoulders, rejoicing. And when he comes home, he calls together his friends and neighbors, saying to them, "Rejoice with me, for I have found my sheep which was lost!" I say to you that likewise there will be more joy in heaven over one sinner who repents than over ninety-nine just persons who need no repentance." Luke 15:4-7

This is a beautiful, personalized picture of God pursuing us in our state of being lost in our wilderness. My own testimony illustrates God finding me in my lost state, not me finding Him. It moves my heart to hear Him celebrate me being found!

In this picture, a shepherd would break the leg of a straying lamb to

12 1 Corinthians 6:19
13 1 Corinthians 3:16

keep it from straying. He would carry the lamb around his neck until the leg healed. In the process of time during the healing, the lamb would come to know the shepherd's voice and even his heartbeat. It is out of our brokenness that God brings healing and intimacy. I know Him! And I am coming to know Him better. I find that I belong personally to my shepherd and that I have great value as "*the one*," but also that I am part of the ninety-nine.

9. **I have been** *sealed in*.
    In Him you also trusted, after you heard the word of truth, the gospel of your salvation; in whom also, having believed, you were sealed with the Holy Spirit of promise, who is the guarantee of our inheritance until the redemption of the purchased possession, to the praise of His glory. Ephesians 1:13-14

This picture is presented as the final one because the message of the picture is so definite. When each of us came to faith, we were sealed in Christ by the Holy Spirit of promise. We have received so much in our salvation relationship, but we still don't have it all. There is more to come, and the Holy Spirit is given to us as a pledge for the future. It is the Holy Spirit indwelling and empowering us who is our guarantee. He also is the one charged with getting us to completion.

> *Being confident of this very thing, that He who has begun a good work in you will complete it until the day of Jesus Christ.* Philippians 1:6

Paul, who wrote these words and gave us the "sealed in" picture from Ephesians spoke with confidence in the power and purpose of God to finish what He started. Jesus was a carpenter. When He started a project, I'm sure it was finished!

There is another aspect of this picture of something being sealed. A king would seal something with his signet, or signature, insuring authentication. A potter would inscribe his mark on the inside bottom of a vessel during the pottery making so you could look in and see who the artist was. God makes His mark on us in a way to authenticate who we belong to. He who has authored us will finish us!

You can see in these pictures that God had to do each of these. We could not do it for ourselves. We did nothing to work our way in. Each picture is a complete picture, not partially done. The context goes from me personally to a community of believers, and each picture could only be undone by the One who did it. Why do I think I have the power or authority to undo something I could never do for myself in the first place?

There is one last picture we should look at. It is different than the fourfold pattern that fits the other pictures, but I believe it is powerful in its simplistic truth. I did a study of God's hands through the Psalms one time, looking at each verse that described his hands, especially as it relates to us. He holds us, He hides us, He protects us, He battles for us, and so on. But in Isaiah, there is a beautiful expression of the use of God's hands:

> But Zion said, "The Lord has forsaken me, and my Lord has forgotten me. "Can a woman forget her nursing child, and not have compassion on the son of her womb? Surely they may forget, yet I will not forget you. See, **I have inscribed you on the palms of My hands;** Your walls are continually before Me. Isaiah 49:14-16

When we feel forgotten by God, He reminds us that we are inscribed on the palms of His hands. Where was Jesus pierced? Is there a connection to the Father's hands and Jesus's hands? So, look at these verses from John 10:

> My sheep hear My voice, and I know them, and they follow Me. And I give them eternal life, and they shall never perish; nei**ther shall anyone snatch them out of my hands.** My Father, who has given them to Me, is greater than all; and **no one is able to snatch them out of My Father's hand.** I and My Father are one. John 10:27-30

We who belong to God are inscribed on His hands. Eternal life is life that will never perish, and no one or nothing can snatch us out of the hands of either the Father or the Son! They are in covenant with each other to hold us in covenant with them!

Back to the question of whether one can lose their salvation. It is a tough question when someone apostatizes (leaves or denies the faith). There are only two possibilities—they either lose what they had, or they never had it. Only God knows for sure, but I personally have modified my position. Eternal life is eternal, it isn't tentative or conditional. I now align myself with my friend's answer. Once in covenant relationship with Him, He keeps us.

Part 3

BECOMING WHO WE ARE

Somewhere I heard the phrase, "be to do"—not "do to be."This little difference is quite profound in the message. Performance oriented Christians *do to be*. They live different in order to be a Christian. Identity oriented Christians *be to do*. They live differently because we are different. This isn't two sides of the same coin; it is two radically different belief systems.

But I added something to the phrase to make it more complete—*be to do,* **do to grow, grow to be.** In other words, we are active participants in our spiritual growth. When we are born again, if we expect to get beyond the infant stage of our new self and get off the bottle to eat the meat, we can't be passive about our growth. The New Testament is full of admonitions and instructions and active verbs that concern our part in our growth. In this section, we'll discuss the process and activities of how we come to maturity.

Chapter 15
"I'M TRYING!"

But you have not so learned Christ, if indeed you have heard
Him and have been taught by Him, as the truth is in Jesus: that
you put off, concerning your former conduct, the old man which
grows corrupt according to the deceitful lusts, and be renewed in
the spirit of your mind, and that you put on the new man which
was created according to God, in true righteousness and holiness.
EPHESIANS 4:20–24

Good, you're trying! Not good, you're trying! Which is it? It's good in the sense that your "want to" is engaged. It's not good in the sense of the "I am" being engaged. After all, "I'm Trying" could be the title for chapter 7 of Romans. Any effort that focuses on self as the source of getting better, doing better, overcoming, etc. will end in frustration. We might even say, *"wretched man that I am!"* The better title than *"I'm Trying,"* would be, *"I'm Abiding."*

> *You are already clean because of the word which I have spoken to*
> *you.* **Abide in Me,** *and I in you. As the branch cannot bear fruit of*
> *itself unless it abides in the vine, so neither can you unless you* **abide**
> **in Me.** *I am the vine, you are the branches;* **he who abides in Me**
> *and* **I in him,** *he bears much fruit, for apart from Me you can do*
> *nothing.* John 15:3-5 (NASB)

Have you ever opened a "requires assembly" product, only to become so frustrated in trying to follow poorly written or illustrated instructions that you just wanted to box it up and send it back? At least now there is probably a *YouTube* video made by someone who figured it out and that wanted to relieve the pain of others.

We are conditioned to being told how to do something. I don't know the number of times I have been asked *"How do you abide in Christ?"* Is it our quiet time? How long does our quiet time have to last? Does it require scripture memory? What do WE do vs. what Christ does? How do I know when I'm abiding and when I'm not? Hmmm...I don't know if I have ever abided, or I would remember it.

Let's back up and uncomplicate it. We were created by God to:

- Have an intimate relationship with Him
- Walk and live and thrive in our new identity in Christ
- Fulfill a purpose God has designed us for
- Live a fruitful life, bearing fruit for His kingdom and His glory
- Reign in life through abiding in Christ

We were designed by God to be fruitful! We are equipped and gifted by God to be fruitful! When we are living His life in us and are bearing fruit, we experience His joy! We don't bear fruit by trying harder. We bear fruit by being who we are and walking in it. How do we know what that looks like for us? That "knowing" comes from abiding in Christ.

This is a prayer Paul prayed for the church at Colossae, which is also a prayer for us:

For this reason we also, since the day we heard it, do not cease to pray for you, and to ask that you may be filled with the knowledge of His will in all wisdom and spiritual understanding; that you may walk worthy of the Lord, fully pleasing Him, being fruitful in every good work and increasing in the knowledge of God; strengthened with all might, according to His glorious power, for all patience and longsuffering with joy; giving thanks to the Father who has qualified us to be partakers of the inheritance of the saints in the light. Colossians 1:9-12

The wrong question is, "How do we abide in Christ?" It isn't a method! The right question is, "What does it mean or what does it look like to abide in Christ? "

The word *abide* means *to be fixed in, to dwell, to live, to remain.*

*Now it happened as they went that He entered a certain village; and a certain woman named Martha welcomed Him into her house. And she had a sister called Mary, who also **sat at Jesus' feet and heard His word. But Martha was distracted** with much serving, and she approached Him and said, "Lord, do You not care that my sister has left me to serve alone? Therefore tell her to help me." And Jesus answered and said to her, **"Martha, Martha, you are worried and troubled about many things. But one thing is needed,** and **Mary has chosen that good part,** which will not be taken away from her."* Luke 10:38-42

Mary chose to abide. Her mindset was to sit at Jesus's feet and receive from Him. At some point, the right thing for her to do would be to get up and serve—to "be fruitful and productive." But first, she must abide. Martha was trying to be fruitful by serving, but she was troubled, distracted, and anxious. *There is a time to receive from Him and a time to serve. We must get it in the right order.* If we get it in the wrong order, we experience what Martha experienced—worry, distraction, and being troubled. We could even say there is abiding for receiving and serving out of abiding.

An example of this order is found in Psalm 1. It teaches us that the man who meditates in scripture will prosper in all he does, because he meditates on God's word. He doesn't meditate because he prospers, he prospers because he meditates.

> *Blessed is the man Who walks not in the counsel of the ungodly, Nor stands in the path of sinners, Nor sits in the seat of the scornful; 2 But his delight is in the law of the LORD, And in His law he meditates day and night. 3 He shall be like a tree Planted by the rivers of water, That brings forth its fruit in its season, Whose leaf also shall not wither; And whatever he does shall prosper.* Psalm 1:1–3

We don't grow apart from our relationship with Christ nor does He cause our growth without our participation. Here is another great scripture that illustrates the togetherness of our participation with Him—

> *Therefore, my beloved, as you have always obeyed, not as in my presence only, but now much more in my absence,* **work out** *your own salvation with fear and trembling; for it is God who* **works in** *you both to will and to do for His good pleasure.* Philippians 2:12–13

The word for us working out is *katergozomai,* which means to keep working toward the goal of finishing something. The word for God working in is *energeo* which is the spiritual life of God at work in us. We work out what He is working in. His work is a mystery, our work is not. What we do is a known, intentional act with a correct attitude and heart. We choose all of those factors, and it isn't complicated. But it is a mystery how God works in us and imparts spiritual life to us, resulting in fruit bearing. We can't control it or manipulate it.

At the beginning of the Sermon on the Mount, we see the established order of the disciples before Jesus:

> *And seeing the multitudes, He went up on a mountain, and when* **He was seated** *His disciples came to Him.* Matthew 5:1

The word for *seated,* or, *"being set,"* is *kathizo,* a word often used to describe judges and other persons of authority taking their seat of authority. I imagine that the disciples learned that when Jesus, usually walking ahead of them, would stop somewhere and sit down that it was "teaching time." I also believe they would eagerly come and sit before him to learn, not wanting to miss a word he said. After they gathered around him and sat before him, they were ready. He begins the beatitudes with the first beatitude, and it's first for a reason. He says, *"Blessed are the poor in spirit, for theirs is the Kingdom of Heaven."*

It is important to understand that there were two words for poor in Greek,—*penes and ptochos.* The *penes* poor can and does something to lift himself from his poverty. But the *ptochos* poor is in abject poverty and cannot rid himself of it. *Ptochos* is the word used in this beatitude. In effect, Jesus is saying, *"Blessed is the man who has come to the end of himself and has given up. The Kingdom belongs to such a one."*

Sitting at Jesus's feet segues into a discussion about abiding in Christ. Abiding is our position *in* Christ and an often-repeated relational concept in the word. We see it 120 times in scripture, and 80 times in John's gospel—15 times in chapter 15 and 31 times in 1 John 1-3.

The beginning of abiding is to choose the place at his feet facing him, poor in spirit, empty and ready to receive, fully surrendered. It is the posture and attitude we choose. We bring a willingness and an openness and an appetite to the relational time with Jesus. We choose the soil of our heart to be fertile. Beyond these things, we don't bring much else to the table.

Abiding is a continued and uninterrupted relationship between Jesus and me. Abiding gives God time and proximity to teach me to listen and hear and to draw on the supply of the Spirit that is accessed through abiding. God is after fruit—not leaves. The DNA for reproductivity is in the seed which is in the fruit. Being fruitful comes from abiding and fruit grows—it isn't produced.

For those who live according to the flesh set their minds on the things of the flesh, but those who live according to the Spirit, the things of the Spirit—Romans 8:5. *I say then: Walk in the Spirit, and you shall not fulfill the lust of the flesh.* Galatians 5:16

Too often we are preoccupied with overcoming the flesh to walk in the Spirit. Our focus is toward the flesh. Our desire is to overcome sin and to be victorious. Our *"want to"* is good, but we fail. We need to reverse the order, as we are taught in Galatians 5:16. *If we walk in the Spirit we will NOT fulfill the lust of the flesh.* Which way are you pointed? If you are facing the flesh to overcome it, your back is to the Spirit. Turn around!

Likewise you also, reckon yourselves to be dead indeed to sin, but alive to God in Christ Jesus our Lord. Therefore do not let sin reign in your mortal body, that you should obey it in its lusts. And do not present your members as instruments of unrighteousness to sin, but present yourselves to God as being alive from the dead, and your members as instruments of righteousness to God. For sin shall not have dominion over you, for you are not under law but under grace. Romans 6:11-14

There may be a time in our spiritual walk when we are learning these truths that we are sin conscious and we're trying to figure out how to deal with the power of sin. But as we learn the truth and know the truth and reckon the truth, then we shift from being *sin conscious* to being *life conscious*. Those who reign in life do not obsess with overcoming sin—it is impossible to do both at the same time.

For if by the one man's offense death reigned through the one, much more those who receive abundance of grace and of the gift of righteousness will reign in life through the One, Jesus Christ.) Romans 5:17

Jesus came that we might have life, and abundantly so. God's intention is for us to live His life abundantly—walking by the Spirit, led by the Spirit, empowered by the Spirit—and not obsessed with overcoming sin. That is why the Spirit lives in us.

Back to abiding. To abide is being in Him as the branch is in the vine. We "rest" in His finished work and cease from our own work.

There remains therefore a rest for the people of God. For he who has entered His rest has himself also ceased from his works as God did from His. Let us therefore be diligent to enter that rest, lest anyone fall according to the same example of disobedience. Hebrews 4:9-11

But abiding is not a passive existence at all. As fruit is growing on the branches, the vine is supplying life. The result is fruit. Leaves are the by-product. Leaves without fruit are worthless. That is why Jesus cursed the fig tree—it was not worth anything.

If abiding is not passive, then there is activity. What does it look like for us to be active? Remember,, *I can **do all things** through Christ who strengthens me.*[14] There are lots of *action verbs* that describe our activity as we rest and abide in Him! We *reach, run, possess, walk, seize, grasp, endure, embrace, forgive,* and so on. Resting in Christ is active!

Abiding in Christ begins with the soil condition of our heart. We must choose for our heart to be good soil, for in making that choice intentionally, we eliminate the bad soil options.

In Matthew's gospel, the *Parable of the Sower* is the first parable Jesus taught:

On the same day Jesus went out of the house and sat by the sea. And great multitudes were gathered together to Him, so that He got into a boat and sat; and the whole multitude stood on the shore. Then He spoke many things to them in parables, saying: "Behold, a sower went out to sow. And as he sowed, some seed fell by the wayside; and the birds came and devoured them. Some fell on stony places, where they did not have much earth; and they immediately sprang up because they had no depth of earth. But when the sun was up they

---

14 Philippians 4:13

*were scorched, and because they had no root they withered away.
And some fell among thorns, and the thorns sprang up and choked
them. But others fell on good ground and yielded a crop: some a
hundredfold, some sixty, some thirty. He who has ears to hear, let
him hear!"* Matthew 13:1–9

I believe this parable has two applications—one describes the range
of responses to salvation and the other is heart preparation for discipleship. Both applications center around the Word of God, and the soil
types fit both.

For *salvation*, the seed that fell on "good ground" brought forth crops
of varying levels. Seed that fell along the wayside or on rocky soil or among
thorns ultimately produced no fruit because the soil conditions did not
permit it. As the Gospel is preached, only people with hearts of "good
ground" who respond are truly saved.

For *discipleship*, fruitful growth occurs when the condition of our
heart to receive the word of God is good ground. How often does the
word fall on rocky soil, where it never takes good root—or is choked
out by the cares and distractions of the world? As followers of Christ,
we determine the condition of our heart at any given time. The "good
ground" is characterized by *openness, eagerness, and focus.*

THE MEANS OF GRACE FOR ABIDING

God's grace gives us the means for our activity of abiding. We do these
"abiding activities" to cultivate, water, nourish, and protect the eternal
seed. It is what we *do* to *grow* (remember: be to do, do to grow, grow to
be). We don't do them to prove anything to God, or to gain His favor
or acceptance. We were spiritually reborn to abide in this relationship.
The means of grace for abiding are what we recognize many times as
spiritual disciplines. *But if we see them as abiding disciplines, they look and
feel different.* Though the following list looks and sounds familiar, open
your heart to see them a little differently.

Rather than reading your Bible, try, interacting with the Word.
The Word is active, living, and powerful. There are many ways to read and study the Word. *The best method is the one a person will actually do*—just like the best translation is the one you will pick up and use. But I have found that in reading your Bible, the most fruitful way is to read it slowly, in small chunks—looking for things you've never noticed and forming thoughts and questions around those newly discovered things. This is a form of scripture meditation. As you read earlier, one of the greatest promises in scripture is in Psalm 1, the promise of what comes from scripture meditation:

> *He shall be like a tree Planted by the rivers of water, That brings forth its fruit in its season, Whose leaf also shall not wither; And whatever he does shall prosper.* Psalm 1:1–3

The word for meditate is *haga*, which means to mutter to yourself, but it also describes how a cow chews its cud! I will spare you the veterinary description of a cow chewing its cud, but it is a mouthful at a time. And if you've ever seen a cow chewing its cud, they are laying down and at peace with the world! It is better to process a small chunk and get more nutrients from it than to swallow lots of undigested scripture.

The Holy Spirit is our teacher in our private reading time, and He delights to show us treasures when we have slowed down enough to get them. Of course, there is value in systematic study or daily reading plans that take you through the whole Bible, but people I know who have tried the slow, little mouthful approach really like it. The Word gets written on our hearts and comes out like a fountain when we have the opportunity to minister to or encourage someone else.

The promise of prospering in every area of your life belongs to the person who is willing to set themselves aside with the living Word of God in this practice of meditation, which is nothing less than sitting at Jesus's feet!

Rather than praying, try having a conversation with your *friend* who is also your *Lord*.

Many years ago, I set aside my prayer list (the long list of people I tried to pray for every day.) I am not saying you should do that necessarily, but consider what prayer is. It is conversation—remembering that Jesus is your friend and is easy to talk to, but He is also Lord. The conversation is somewhat casual, but it always goes somewhere that He directs. We talk, but we also *do a lot of listening*. Praying for our needs (petition) and for others (intercession) in the context of a conversation means we are doing a lot of listening.

I'm a huge advocate for journaling. I almost hesitate to say that because some people are turned off at the suggestion of writing something that might look like a diary. But something happens in our mind when we write. Thoughts are completed, visual ideas emerge, and it slows us enough to hear God's voice.

I personally begin my prayer time with thanksgiving—every time—whether I am journaling or not. Thanksgiving does two things—it sets my attitude in the right frame of mind, and it establishes His lordship in my life. What about praying for my needs? It gets very personal and honest. Sometimes, I will ask the Lord, *"How am I doing?"* That opens the subject quite wide, and He will answer. I love talking to the Lord about my emotions and circumstances, and problems and questions. I receive direction, encouragement, and even empowerment—those are things which come from abiding prayer. What about praying for others? Oh yes—intercession happens a lot but in a conversational context. I love to hear from the Lord on someone's behalf. It is always an encouragement to pass on.

How long do I pray? Well, that depends. When I sit at His feet, I try to stay until He says it's time to get up. Not everyone has that flexibility in their schedule and many days I don't either, but if I approach it in the right mindset, it works—whether I end up in fifteen minutes of prayer or an hour.

**Rather than fellowship with other Christians, try the idea of
chaverim.**

Chaver is the Hebrew word for friend and when you add the *im*, it makes
it plural. The idea is that everyone needs one or more friends who can take
you higher and deeper and that you also are that type of friend to others.

As Jesus grew up, he learned from His parents, from His synagogue,
from gatherings of men and their sons, and of course from His own time
with the Father and the Holy Spirit. He learned from all those sources,
being fully human. But during Jesus's years at home in Nazareth, the men
and older sons would gather as *chaverim* in informal settings, usually in
the evenings. It provided the opportunity to learn from each other. Close
relationships and small groups where everyone learn from each other,
and everyone is a contributor is far superior to the classroom lecture
approach. More learning takes place in good small groups than from ser-
mons preached on Sundays. Whether it is small group ministry or informal friendship gatherings, be intentional about helping each other grow.

**Rather than witnessing to others, consider the principle of
planting seed, watering, and providing sunshine, and of
multiplying and reproducing.**

After all, "be fruitful and multiply" is the first command given to Adam
and Eve. Some people are wired for cold call evangelism to strangers. Most
of us aren't. But if we expand our thinking a bit and consider that *who
we are* has the capacity to be reproduced in others, then we might start
noticing the many opportunities before us to do that very thing. Being
fruitful and multiplying has an order. You multiply (reproduce) the fruitfulness of your life. Sometimes that results in someone else being born
again but often you are ministering life and encouragement to a believer.

Many of us have had the experience of reading or meditating on
scripture and we have that exciting *"Aha!"* moment of seeing something
for the first time. We believe the Holy Spirit just downloaded some new

illumination for us personally, often related to something we're going through. We call that the *rhema* word, the *heard word* of God visited upon us to encourage or help us in the moment. What a great feeling that is! But when we excitedly tell someone else it doesn't have that effect on them at all! It's as though it hits the ground before it gets to their heart!

When this happens, it might be that when the word came to us it tasted like ripe fruit—so good! But we ingest it in seed form in that moment and before we can feed it to someone else it needs to grow from seed to ripe fruit inside of us, which takes time, meditation , and the cultivation of the seed. Multiplying follows fruitfulness. Fruitfulness comes from abiding.

> *I am the vine, you are the branches. He who abides in Me, and I in him, bears much fruit; for without Me you can do nothing—* John 15:5.

Paul understood that spiritual formation that comes from abiding. But he also had a passion for reproduction:

> *My little children, for whom **I labor in birth again** until Christ is formed in you—*Galatians 4:19.

You can hear the emotion of his passion for the fruitfulness of them growing into maturity and he took it as a personal charge to see that formation take place. Of course, it was Paul who said, "you have many teachers but not many fathers." Teachers do a great service to the local church in discipling, but fathers reproduce others. Reproduction is the highest form of discipleship in the church.

Rather than going to church, consider being in love with what/who Christ loves.

*Husbands, love your wives, just as **Christ also loved the church** and gave Himself for her, that **He might sanctify and cleanse her** with the washing* *of water by the word, that He* **might present her to Himself a glorious church, not having spot or wrinkle** *or any such thing, but that she should be holy and without blemish.* Ephesians 5:25-27

Jesus loves the church as she is, just as He loves us as we are. But He loves us too much to not want the best for us. So, despite our spots and wrinkles, we are loved and accepted and He by no means is giving up on us. He is after a glorious church. The point here is to love what Jesus loves, which for us is *our local version of His bride.* Be certain that you are in the local church He planted you in and then stay the course.

Rosanne and I have been a part of Trinity Fellowship since its beginning. In forty-six years, there have been countless reasons to leave, but that is the wrong train of thought. It isn't, *"Why should we leave?"* There are always reasons to leave. The question is, *"Why are we staying?"* There are times that God transplants people into a different local bride. But most people who change churches do so for self-centered or self-referenced reasons, such as being hurt, offended, disappointed, or disillusioned—not because God told them to go.

Churches are relational gatherings of people with problems and hurts and expectations, so the soil for offense is always fertile. You could even say that churches are breeding grounds for offenses because expectations are so high. You WILL be hurt in church, guaranteed! But being hurt doesn't mean you will be damaged. How we respond to hurt determines whether it is damaging. Extinguish those offenses before they become bitter. You can do this!

So, stay on the course! I have prayed the Psalm 139 prayer more times than I can count. *Search me, O God, and know my heart; Try me, and know my anxieties; And see if there is any wicked way in me And lead me in the way everlasting.*

No matter what trial I was going through caused by someone else, between me and God it was all about what He wanted to do in my heart because there is always something there that needs to be tended to. We are each living stones being built into His holy temple. It takes time and chiseling for stones to fit together.

Rather than tithing, consider loving and worshipping God with your giving.

I know there are different views about tithing in the New Testament. I believe in tithing though my paradigm might be a little different than some. Tithing came before the law, with Abraham tithing to Melchizedek (the references in Hebrews tell me it still exists in the New Testament). But Abraham gave a tithe following the blessing Melchizedek gave to him. As New Covenant believers, we give our tithes and offerings as an act of worship for the blessing of life in Christ. We love to give and always have. When we give, it is with deep gratitude and a heart of worship. More could be said and argued over regarding principles of giving, but we LOVE to give to Him who gives to us. And I've learned many times over that you can't outgive God.

Giving does three things—it connects you to God through worship; it tells God you trust Him; it connects you to a community and a vision that people can't do on their own. Better together, as they say.

Rather than worshiping, consider entering in, clothed in humility.

*Therefore, brethren, having boldness **to enter the Holiest by the blood of Jesus**, by a new and living way which He consecrated for us, through the veil, that is, His flesh, and having a High Priest over the house of God, let us draw near with a true heart in **full assurance of faith**, having our hearts sprinkled from an evil conscience and our bodies washed with pure water. Let us hold fast the confession of our hope without wavering, for He who promised is faithful. And let us **consider one another** in order to stir up love and good works, **not forsaking the assembling of ourselves together**, as is the manner of some, but exhorting one another, and so much the more as you see the Day approaching.* Hebrews 10:19–25

Worship is not just singing praise choruses, as awesome as many of them are. It is a chosen movement and posture into His presence. We intentionally move toward Him. In Israel, a favorite site we visit is at Chorazin, where the remains of the village have been excavated, including a synagogue. When you approach the entrance of this synagogue from the south, you notice that the steps going up are of different heights. Our guide explained to us that this is intentional, so that you are forced to bow your head to go up, in order not to stumble.

Of course, humility is of the heart, not the position of the head, but the architecture teaches us something of the worship of ancient Israel. They understood that humility is a choice and is intentional. You don't accidentally humble yourself! We enter His gates with thanksgiving and His courts with praise. A thankful heart is your path through the gate. Again, this is a choice. Even in seasons of pruning, there is so much to be thankful for.

Though you can worship by yourself, it is not a substitute for community worship. Ancient Israel worshipped God in community in almost every instance. God loves to meet with His people. Sometimes the transformation we need most comes in a community worship setting.

Rather than taking a Sabbath day off, consider piddling the day away!

Space does not allow for a thorough discussion of abiding and sabbath rest. But we need to know that the sabbath did not end with the passing of the Old Covenant. Sabbath preceded the law. Jesus is Lord of the Sabbath and brings fulfilling meaning to it. We see by His life that He was very active on the Sabbath. Most of His confrontation with the religious authorities was concerning the miracles He performed on the Sabbath. I think He intentionally waited until the Sabbath to perform some of them!

So how do we talk about Sabbath rest in the context of this chapter on abiding? I recommend an excellent book on the subject by Mark Buchanan called, "*The Rest of God*." I read this book during a very stressful time in my life. We were in the middle of a major facility expansion at Trinity that I was overseeing, and I could hardly sleep at night with all the management details continually racing through my mind. One night the Lord woke me and cautioned me that if I didn't change my rhythm, I would do emotional and physical damage to myself. It was a warning, and I took it seriously!

Within a few days I was told about this book by Mark Buchanan. I credit the book to getting some understanding about a very misunderstood topic—Sabbath for the New Covenant believer. I won't try to summarize the book, but I will lay out a few principles that I have incorporated into my life.

There is a time to *cease* what we are doing and stay ceased for a time and it should be regular. The most difficult thing for driven people to do is to cease, especially in our American culture. We are measured and affirmed for productivity and achievement. To take a day per week that nothing is measured, and achievement is off the table, is antithetical to how we think! But that is what Sabbath does—it breaks up the rhythm of producing so we can walk in a new rhythm of resting. Our rest might be very active, but it shouldn't be productive, at least not measured! For me, Sabbath is an intentional break in routine and an entering into a restful abiding. It is a time for reflection and even creativity. The key is that the day is different. I offer the word "*piddle*" as a way of expressing my Sabbath. I piddle on the Sabbath. Piddling requires no planning or execution or measurement. But piddling is very relaxing and refreshing and replenishing, and sometimes even creative. Have a good *piddle day* and read the book—I recommend it!

These means of grace for abiding represent the rhythm of God in YOUR life. Indulge in ALL of them—not some of them. Consider it a balanced diet. These are but some of the means of grace for abiding—there are others. You can add your own to the list. Anything that intentionally draws you in to more intimacy with Him is on your list.

Are you so foolish? Having begun in the Spirit, are you now being made perfect by the flesh? Galatians 3:3

We began in the Spirit, and it is in the Spirit that we will be completed!

Chapter 16

COMMUNITY LIFE: THE ME BECOMES WE

I, therefore, the prisoner of the Lord, beseech you to walk worthy
of the calling with which you were called, with all lowliness and
gentleness, with longsuffering, bearing with one another in love,
endeavoring to keep the unity of the Spirit in the bond of peace.
There is one body and one Spirit, just as you were called in one
hope of your calling; one Lord, one faith, one baptism; one God and
Father of all, who is above all, and through all, and in you all.
EPHESIANS 4:1–6

Fred and Sally (fictitious persons), have two children, ages seven and ten. They have attended the same church since their oldest was a baby. They chose their church because they had friends their age that recommended it, and the nursery was well staffed and clean and safe. All was well until a few simultaneous bumps in the road. Sally was a part of a women's life group that she really liked. It was made up mostly of young mothers like herself and she became close friends with some of the other mothers. Some of those friendships took a wrong turn and Sally found herself outside of their circle, wondering what she did wrong.

Fred was not in a life group, but he had become friends with some of the men from the same circle of young couples. He became offended that his wife was excluded from her circle. Their children were very busy with sports and other activities, many of which took up time on the weekends, including Sundays. At first, Fred and Sally were conflicted about the competition for their time and energy and the impact it was having on church involvement. But with the relational problems developing, it became a relief to choose sports activities instead of church.

As a family, they began drifting. Drifting from church also meant drifting in their spiritual life as well. Eventually, Fred and Sally and their kids became part of the de-churched crowd. Or maybe they decided to start over in a new church. This fictitious story is very real and happens over and over in churches everywhere. Change the names and the circumstances and you have the most frustrating situation that pastors face every day.

Every church has a back door, and the challenge of every church is keeping it closed as much as possible. Why do people leave churches? Sometimes people join the de-churched crowd. The COVID-19 pandemic left behind a large contingent of people who never came back. More often people leave one church to go to another. Unfortunately, many people have a mindset about churches like they do their living room furniture. When the cat scratches the fabric or they just want a change—a new look and feel—it is time to be out with the old and in with the new.

What does the Bible have to say about the subject? There are a lot of instructions about how to resolve relational problems—*forgiving one another, showing mercy and kindness, building up each other*, etc. Those admonitions are there because churches are relational environments where expectations are very high about how people should treat each other. That is why churches are breeding grounds for offenses.

Our pastoral team at Trinity Fellowship works on the problem of the back door constantly. Using technology, we can better track the leavers so that personal contact can be made to resolve any issues they might have. Those follow up conversations are often very fruitful. Sometimes they aren't. But there is no question that the heart of God is for people to stay planted in one place for a long time so they can bloom. Sometimes God will move someone after they have been trained and discipled and made ready for a new assignment. But most people don't leave churches or change churches for that reason. They leave because they are disappointed, or hurt, or offended, or neglected, or—you can fill in the blank! Perhaps the better question than, "Why do people leave," is, "Why are they not staying?" There are always reasons to leave. But people who stay have their reasons for doing so, and they are usually solid.

In our chapter on the biblical pictures of our salvation, the *me* becomes *we* immediately. At least as far as God is concerned, it does. Our new and wonderful normal is to be in a community of believers in a functional and fruit producing status. This is true for all believers, regardless of their level of maturity. Let's discuss two levels of believers—new believers and mature believers, knowing that the spectrum is wide between the two. Remember, we are all complete *(pleroo)* becoming mature *(telios)*. We are all on a journey together moving in the same direction.

New believers are usually more open and excited to share with non-believers about their salvation experience. New believers bring an enthusiasm to a group that refreshes everyone in the joy of their salvation. New believers remind us of our beginning and early times of spiritual growth. New believers cause us to revisit the roots and beginnings of our faith. New believers need milk, but they need to progress to solid food. For that to happen effectively, there has to be intentional discipleship from more mature believers. It is misguided and very inadequate to expect new believers to get it on their own.

When we are baptized into Christ for our salvation (which water baptism illustrates), we immediately are clothed with the newness of Christ. We are raised with Him as a new self, a new person, a new man. We are sanctified and made clean, having been given a new identity. We are adopted into sonship and given by Christ to the Father. The Holy Spirit indwells us and empowers us to begin living our new life. We become a saint, singular, and saints, plural with all other born-again believers. We don't have any choice in the matter of becoming a part of the body of Christ. The most common biblical word to describe us as believers plural, is *brethren*.

The word for brethren is *adelphos*, meaning *unity of the womb*. We all become children of God out of the same spiritual rebirth experience. We came out of the same womb! Just as in natural life we don't get to choose who our siblings are, the same is true in our spiritual life. Though we choose which local church we're a part of, we soon find out who our immediate siblings are in that local community. And what we find out is that we have some fellow saints that we are drawn to and those that are irritating. Sadly, many people choose churches over and over, looking for the one that suits them the best. Or they choose to go it alone. So, in this chapter, we are considering several important characteristics and challenges for the Body and Bride of Christ of which we are a part.

CHURCH IS GOD'S PLAN, NOT MAN'S.

At each of the three Trinity campuses I have served as pastor, I always obsessed over the spiritual wellbeing of members and families. Shepherds with a pastoral heart will do that. A well led church with a strong leadership team and an active congregation deploying the variation of their giftings will be a church that prospers. Said again in fewer words—a healthy church will be a growing church. God can and will add people to that church.

CHURCH

The Bible gives us several pictures of church: the community of believers, the brethren (*adelphos*), local congregations, sheep with a shepherd(s), living stones being built into a spiritual house, the body of Christ, and branches in the vine are all biblical pictures of us together. This is God's plan. Church was His idea, and the local church is our place to make it happen. So, we have a responsibility to accept it, love it, nurture it, and take care of it.

> *Husbands, love your wives, just as Christ also loved the church and gave Himself for her, that He m**ight sanctify and cleanse her with the washing of water by the word**, that He might present her to Himself a glorious church, **not having spot or wrinkle** or any such thing, but that she should be holy and without blemish.* Ephesians 5:25–27

We love what Christ loved and gave His life for. Why would we think we have an option? Rosanne and I have been a part of the same church for more than forty years. In this church we have been hurt, rejected, overlooked, neglected, and deeply disappointed many times. Our children have been hurt many times as well. But in this same church, we have been cared for, loved, accepted, taught, discipled, trained and blessed beyond description. In any relational setting, things don't always go your way. And sometimes they do go your way.

So why did we stay? After all, there are a lot of good churches to choose from. The main reason we stayed is we have skin in the game. Our fingerprints are on this place and the fingerprints of others are on us. We have history and heritage and legacy. But it takes time and perseverance for those things to develop.

CHRISTIAN COMMUNITY

Everyone is somewhere on a discipleship journey toward marks of spiritual maturity. I use the plural form of marks because a person can be mature in some areas of their Christian walk and less mature in other areas. In a healthy functioning church, the progression should generally be from being discipled by others to taking responsibility for our own growth to reproducing our maturity in others. The Apostle Paul took discipleship very seriously. The following two scriptures are examples of many that demonstrate his commitment to nurturing others to maturity.

> *Brethren, join in following my example, and note those who so walk, as you have us for a pattern.* Philippians 3:17

> *My little children, for whom I labor in birth again until Christ is formed in you* Galatians 4:19

The world has just been through an experience that we are still trying to understand—the COVID -19 pandemic. Everyone was affected by it. We didn't see it coming, we didn't know what to do, and we are still wondering what happened on some level and will be for a long time to come. The pandemic is supposedly over, but its effects will be around for a long time. Churches certainly were impacted. Church gatherings of all types were suspended for various lengths of time. Trinity Fellowship had a strong technology capacity and was able to have an online platform almost immediately. Our online attendance during the weeks we were not meeting was strong. When we resumed in person gatherings, we kept our online services going. In person attendance has gradually risen but is still catching up to what it was before the pandemic. The combination between in person and online attendance is higher than pre-pandemic numbers, but *online attenders are missing something.*

What are they missing? Community—something we call the three-feet effect, representing the effect people have on each other who are within arm's length. Technology is wonderful, but it can't solve the problem of relational distance. Some things don't change, and the church has always needed this arm's length relational connectivity. We need to get into the personal space of others and they in ours. How else can we get at the spots and wrinkles?

At the Last Supper, Jesus shocked the disciples by washing their feet. It was so extraordinary, that He gave them an explanation for what He had done.

> *So when He had washed their feet, taken His garments, and sat down again, He said to them, "Do you know what I have done to you? You call Me Teacher and Lord, and you say well, for so I am. If I then, your Lord and Teacher, have washed your feet,* **you also ought to wash one another's feet. For I have given you an example, that you should do as I have done to you**. John 13:12–15

On the one hand, He was speaking of relational humility and how they were to prefer one another and not compete for status, privilege, or honor. But was He also speaking of something else?

In the biblical world, people walked everywhere and seldom on paved roads. The dirtiest part of their body was their feet as it was covered with the dust of the world. Washing one another's feet is a spiritual metaphor for helping our brothers and sisters take off the effect of living in this fallen world. Every time you pray for someone or encourage someone you are taking some dust off. We all need this. Community is an essential part of walking out and living our life in Christ.

When should I consider changing churches?

There are legitimate reasons for changing churches. I encourage people new to Trinity to "date us" for a while before you decide to get married to us, because church membership should be almost that serious. The first rule of thumb is that a local church should be a good fit. Churches of different sizes fit differently for different people. Churches have different personalities and missions. It is very important to be part of a church that has a solid Statement of Faith and that is grounded in the authority of God's Word. Another important fit is that the church works reasonably well for your family. But that can also be a slippery slope. Be wary of changing churches because there is conflict with your teenager and others in the youth group; or your teenager's friends attend a different church; or your elementary age student is bored and has lost interest. There is no perfect arrangement that meets all the family's needs, but there are a lot of churches that are working diligently to do well, and it could be that your involvement is to be part of the solution.

Earlier in this book, in the sharing of my testimony, I told of the time I spent six months in a cult. Not only was it a dangerous time for me personally, being so young in faith, but it was a critically important time for me to learn about the necessity of good, healthy, strong leadership in a local church. I believe the church we choose should be a safe and healthy church with good, solid church government. Space does not permit a discussion of all the elements that go into good church government, but a church that is not well-led by a strong leadership team can very easily go sideways and create an unsafe church.

There are other factors that can make a church unhealthy, but good government and protocols can solve those problems. If you are in a healthy church, stay there. If you are in an unhealthy church, check out the prospects of the church leadership's potential of solving those problems. If it looks hopeless or marginal for change, it may be time to move on. The best grid for this is that God has equipped you in one place to serve in another, and the leadership agrees with the change.

GENERATIONS

Trinity Fellowship is a forty-six-year-old church at the time of this writing. When it began in 1977, I was twenty-four years old. The "older" people in the original group were in their early to mid-thirties. We were all young. It is remarkable that we did as well as we did! Figuring out how to start and build a church without a senior generation there to guide us was not easy. But figure it out we did, as we relied on the Holy Spirit to guide us. The generation that started Trinity is the generation that stayed the course and was instrumental in laying the foundations and contending through the hard times to build a significant kingdom impacting local church with a worldwide reach and influence. Many churches have done what we did or even exceeded it, but it has been a joy to have been a part of Trinity since the beginning.

About fifteen years ago, as we moved into a major facility expansion, we faced three of the most difficult and challenging years in our history. We experienced two leadership transition failures, we were in a financial crisis, and many other things went through a shaking. On the surface, there was some doubt whether Trinity would survive. But underneath the surface, three things emerged that became evident that we would do better than survive—we would thrive at an unprecedented level.

First, our DNA was clear and solid. Who we were on the inside was who we had always been and would always be—a faith-filled body of believers who were Spirit centered and biblically grounded and who wanted everything God had for us. Second, our government was strong and getting wiser with every challenge we went through. We had been tested many times and passed the tests, learning and growing with each experience. Third, we were now a generational church. We had outgrown the original generation who started Trinity, and we clearly had an Abraham, Isaac, and Jacob presence. For the past fifteen years we have been on a learning curve as to how that works.

Each of these three generations has a seat. Can you imagine a church without Abrahams? Or without Jacobs? Trinity Fellowship has a very healthy distribution of age ranges in all three generations. How that works is the subject of another book, but for it to work successfully, a church must be very intentional. It goes far beyond having ministries that minister to each generation. In fact, generations isolated from each other within those ministries can be damaging. A healthy church is committed to generations who are connected to each other in meaningful, relational contexts. That, my friends, is the heart of God!

Chapter 17

WHEN LIFE IS HARD: GLORY TO GLORY

Therefore, having been justified by faith, we have peace with God through our Lord Jesus Christ, through whom also we have access by faith into this grace in which we stand, and rejoice in hope of the glory of God. And not only that, but we also glory in tribulations, knowing that tribulation produces perseverance; and perseverance, character; and character, hope. Now hope does not disappoint, because the love of God has been poured out in our hearts by the Holy Spirit who was given to us.
ROMANS 5:1–5

This final chapter is at the end for a reason. The tone of this book has been very positive and encouraging. The Good News about who Jesus is and what He has done and who you are as a result is truly good news! What is possible for us is incredible!

Though we have spoken frankly that we have opposition from external sources (the world and Satan) and internal opposition (flesh and self) to contend with, our victory is assured. We *can* have authority over sin. We *can* go on to spiritual maturity. We *can* know God intimately and we *can* go on to spiritual maturity. We *can* be so Jesus focused that we reign in life and live in the freedom and power we have in Christ. We *can* know our true identity and by knowing the truth we *can* be set free, and we *can* discern the enemy's lies.

We *can* live and function productively in our faith community and we *can* build up one another in our faith. We *can* know the will of God for our lives and walk in the peace that brings. We *can* share the good news with others and be used by God to plant and water seed and we *can* see God bring the increase as others are born again.

We *can* forgive others when wronged and we *can* help broken relationships be reconciled. We *can* be a part of a leadership team, helping our local church become healthy and strong. We *can* have strong families that are Christ centered. We *can* have children who love the Lord and who commit their lives to Him. We *can* learn to abide in Christ and practice life giving disciplines that cause growth and maturity.

We *can* share the life of Christ with others. We *can* teach and impart truths to others that are imparted to us. We *can* make a difference in the lives of others. We *can* disciple others and reproduce who Christ has made us to be because we *can* give away freely what we have freely received.

The list could go on and on. Lots of "cans" tells us that with God all things are possible. "I *can* do all things *through* Christ who strengthens me." You don't see the word *can't* in any of the above paragraphs! Our life in Christ has limitless possibilities and though we grow older in these earthly tents, our attitude should always be reaching for more.

But sometimes life is hard. Sometimes it is very hard. Two words found often in the Bible are perseverance and endurance which are seldom on anyone's list of favorite words. Because we live in a fallen world and we do have an adversary, we have opposition. Sometimes we make poor or foolish decisions when we reap what we have sown. Sometimes we allow broken relationships to become more broken rather than be healed. Sometimes we intentionally hurt or control or manipulate people. Sometimes people do that to us. Sometimes hard things happen that there is no explanation for. Yes, life can be hard.

We all face adversity and adversity makes us wiser and stronger.

My brethren, count it all joy when you fall into various trials, know-ing that the testing of your faith produces patience. But let patience have its perfect work, that you may be perfect and complete, lacking nothing. If any of you lacks wisdom, let him ask of God, who gives to all liberally and without reproach, and it will be given to him. James 1:2–5

This is but one of many passages that tell us adversity makes us better. Medical doctors will tell you that it is not the routine cases that make them better doctors, but the perplexing ones.

When adversity hits, turn into the wind where the resistance is against you, because it is in facing the wind that the Holy Spirit will fill your sails. Plant your feet, keep moving, and stay the course. Diligence and faithfulness are your half of the scriptural admonition, *"I can do all things through Christ who strengthens me!"* When fatigue sets in, surrender more, don't turn to performance. Remembrance is powerful. Remember all the times when God was faithful. He will do it again! Finally, rejoice and give thanks through the duration of the trial.

There are many scriptures that speak to this subject and in fact, this chapter could be a book. But I choose here to use one more passage that I think helps us to keep a healthy perspective:

But we all, with unveiled face, beholding as in a mirror the glory of the Lord, are being transformed into the same image from glory to glory, just as by the Spirit of the Lord. 2 Corinthians 3:18

This very important scripture is skipped over by many people in their reading because it looks a bit complicated. But if we break it down a little it becomes very descriptive and encouraging. So, let's look at this together.

We all—everyone who is in relationship with Christ. You are included. This is speaking about you!

With unveiled face—the rest of the passage refers to the veil Moses wore so he would not be destroyed by seeing God's face. That veil has been removed in Christ. We don't have a veil. We can see God's face!

Beholding as in a mirror the glory of the Lord—we look in a mirror and see a reflection. It looks like Jesus. It looks like us. It looks like us becoming like Jesus!

Are being transformed into the same image—I just said it—we are being changed or transformed. The word in Greek is *metamorphoo*. A real transformation takes place. It isn't just appearance, it is substance!

From glory to glory—what is that? I heard a teacher illustrate glory to glory many years ago. It was so encouraging and made so much sense, I've never forgotten it. His illustration of glory to glory was a series of ascending, connected circles. He started with one circle and drew another connecting the bottom of the next circle to the top of the previous one. He kept doing that until there were several circles and the last circle on his whiteboard was much higher than the first one. The circles represent glories. Life moves us through seasons that feel like we go up or down as in peaks and valleys. But we move from the top of one circle (a peak—an easy time) to the bottom of the next one (a valley—a hard time). In time, through endurance and faithfulness and forging of character, we move to the top of that circle (back to an easy time). But get ready! The next move is to the bottom of the next circle. The whole time, we are becoming more Christ-like, not through peaks and valleys but from one glory to the next glory, and the glories ascend on an upward trajectory! It might look something like this:

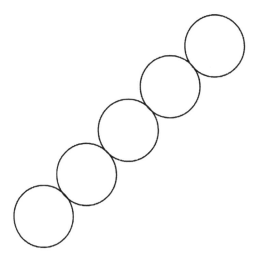

How many glories does a person go through in a lifetime? Of course, there's no way of knowing that, but be encouraged that these trials and tests that you persevere through and learn from and grow from, make you more like Jesus along the way. Your character is being forged. Your wisdom is growing. And the fragrance of Christ coming from you is getting stronger. One of the best things that will ever be said about you is that you smell like Jesus!

POSTSCRIPT

Living the extraordinary life God has for you begins with a right and true understanding of who you are in Him. Identity is key. There is a true identity for you. That means there is a false one. Knowing your true identity doesn't guarantee you will live up to it as there is more to it, as we've seen through these chapters. But it does begin with knowing, then reckoning (believing) and then presenting yourself to God according to that right knowledge and as an act of your will to obey. It really works! On the contrary, a person who doesn't know who they are or who believes a lie about their identity (as in saint vs. sinner), is destined to live according to what they believe. It begins with knowledge. Jesus said, *"You shall know the truth and the truth shall make you free!"*[15]

In a recent conversation with a friend, he asked me about the two greatest commandments, *"to love the Lord your God with All your heart, and to love your neighbor as yourself."*[16] He was wondering about the loving yourself part and asked for my thoughts. And here was my answer:

I love my redeemed self! Why wouldn't I? I'm bought and paid for and completely forgiven. I've been made new, a new creation in Christ. I've been born again of incorruptible seed. I've been regenerated and I've been given the righteousness of Christ. I've been sanctified and I'm

---

15 John 8:32
16 Matthew 22:36-40

growing up into that sanctification, so that I look and act and smell more like Jesus each day. I've been sealed into Christ with the Holy Spirit of promise for all that is yet to come. I am an overcomer in Him and I'm a living stone being built into a holy house with other believers. I am the temple of the Holy Spirit. God lives in me because He has made this clay vessel clean! I am adopted into sonship, and I've been baptized into the body of Christ. I've been transferred from darkness into the kingdom of the glorious, risen Christ! Yes! I love my redeemed self! And it is my redeemed self that can love others the way God wants them to be loved. Sometimes life is hard, but I have a great, glorious life and future. Yes, I am reigning in life, just what Jesus wants for me...and what He wants for you, too. Praise be to Him!

ACKNOWLEDGMENTS

In the preparation of the manuscript, I am grateful for the valuable input of Phil King, D'Les Dyer, and Jori Buchenau. Their input made this book better and more readable. And I am deeply indebted to Bree Proffitt, whose skill, insight, and dedication turned a manuscript into a book. Without her, this would not have happened. I am also grateful to my son David for the cover photos. His creative giftedness is such a blessing to me.

In the subject area of grace and our identity in Christ, one of the books that impacted me early on was *Birthright* by David Needham. My friend Clark Witten and his book *Pure Grace*, as well as other grace writers such as John Sheasby and Andrew Wommack, were very helpful. My friend Darrell Feemster introduced me to some older, classical writers on grace and identity such as W. Ian Thomas, Norman Grubb, Bob George, and L.E. Maxwell. But the book that helped me the most to untie the religious knots and help me get a breakthrough understanding of my identity in Christ was "The Normal Christian Life" by Watchman Nee.

In the development of my understanding of grace, I am grateful to Clark Whitten and Darrell Feemster, whose friendships helped me grow immensely in my faith. My many, long discussions with John Ingerson on our drives to the ranch helped me see things more clearly.

I am very grateful to Pastors Jimmy Evans and Jimmy Witcher, who have mentored me and encouraged me and helped me to become a better pastor and leader.

I am also indebted to the faith community that I have been a part of for the past forty-six years. Men and women whom I have had the privilege of *walking with, studying with, arguing with, and learning with* have been the greatest treasures I could ever hope for. There are too many names to mention, but the men's life group I led for many years and a group of young men (my sons and their friends) who met in my home for years top the list.

Most of all, I am grateful for my family—my wife Rosanne and my children, Tricia, David, Hannah, and Jonathan, and their spouses, and my nine grandchildren, have motivated me more than anyone to reach for God's highest and best and to always have a reason for pressing on. I have been very blessed, indeed.

BIBLIOGRAPHY

Fowler, James. (2005) *Man—As God Intended*, C I Y Publishing

Fowler, James. (2005) *Union With Christ*, C I Y Publishing

Fowler, James. (2005) *Christ at Work In You*, C I Y Publishing

George, Bob. (1989) *Classic Christianity*, Harvest House

Maxwell, L. E. (2010) *Born Crucified*, Moody Publishers

Mumford, Bob. (2002) *Agape Road*, Destiny Image

Nee, Watchman. (1977) *The Normal Christian Life*, Tyndale House

Needham, David. (1979) *Birthright—Christian, Do You Know Who You Are?* Multnomah

Smith, Malcolm. (2002) *The Power of The Blood Covenant*, Harrison House

Thomas, Major W. Ian. (1961) *The Saving Life of Christ*, Zondervan

Thomas, Major W. Ian. (2006) *The Indwelling Life of Christ*, Multnomah

Whitten, Clark. (2012) *Pure Grace*, Destiny Image

Williams, David J. (1999) *Paul's Metaphors—Their Context and Character*, Hendrickson

Wright, N.T. (2005) *Paul*, Fortress Press

ABOUT THE AUTHOR

Bo has 30 years of full-time ministry experience at Trinity Fellowship Church in Amarillo, Texas, where he has most recently served as Executive Pastor of Pastoral Development. Bo and his wife Rosanne are also founding members of Trinity and have been part of its more than 40-year heritage from the beginning. Bo loves to study and teach the scriptures  and is a sought-after mentor to young leaders as they journey to know Christ. His spiritual influence spans multiple generations.

Before entering full-time ministry, Bo served in Amarillo for twenty years as an elementary school teacher, principal, and Central Office Administrator.

Bo and Rosanne have been married for more than 45 years. They have four married children, two sons and two daughters, and nine grandchildren.

Made in the USA
Columbia, SC
07 May 2024